On Mind and Thought

J. Krishnamurti

EastWest Books (Madras) Pvt. Ltd.,
• Chennai • Bangalore • Hyderabad • New Delhi

EastWest Books (Madras) Pvt. Ltd.,

571, Poonamalle High Road, Aminjikarai, Chennai - 600 029.
E-mail : ewb@touchtelindia.net
3-5-1108, Maruti Complex, II Floor, Narayanaguda, Hyderabad - 500 029.
53/2, Bull Temple Road, Basavangudi, Bangalore - 560 019.
A-10, Lower Ground Floor, Lajpat Nagar III, New Delhi - 110 024.

ON MIND AND THOUGHT Copyright © 1993 by
Krishnamurti Foundation Trust Ltd and Krishnamurti Foundation of America

Series editor: Mary Cadogan
Associate editors: Ray McCoy and David Skitt

First EastWest Books paperback edition 2004

For additional information about Krishnamurti Schools, Centres
and other publications contact:
Krishnamurti Foundation Trust Ltd
Brockwood Park, Bramdean, Hampshire, SO24 0LQ, England
E-mail: info@brockwood.org.uk Website: www.kfoundation.org
or
Krishnamurti Foundation of America
P.O. Box 1560, Ojai, California 93024-1560, U.S.A.
E-mail: kfa@kfa.org Website: www.kfa.org
or
Krishnamurti Foundation India
Vasanta Vihar, 124/126 Greenways Road, RA Puram, Chennai - 600 028, India
E-mail: kfihq@md2.vsnl.net.in Website: www.kfionline.org

ISBN : 81-88661-22-8

Cover design J. Menon

Printed at Sri Venkatesa Printing House, Chennai 600 026
E.mail: saicure@vsnl.com

Intelligence is not the clever pursuit of argument, of opposing contradictions, opinions—as though through opinions truth can be found, which is impossible—but it is to realize that the activity of thought, with all its capacities, subtleties and extraordinary ceaseless activity, is not intelligence.

Brockwood Park, 4 September 1982

On Mind and Thought

Other books by J. Krishnamurti from HarperSanFrancisco

Contents

ix   *Foreword*

1   Seattle, 23 July 1950

3   London, 7 April 1952

6   Rajghat, 23 January 1955

10   Rajghat, 6 February 1955

11   Ojai, 21 August 1955

15   Rajghat, 25 December 1955

16   Bombay, 28 February 1965

18   From *The Only Revolution*

21   Saanen, 23 July 1970

27   Saanen, 26 July 1970

34   Saanen, 18 July 1972

41   Saanen, 20 July 1972

52   Brockwood Park, 9 September 1972

55   Saanen, 15 July 1973

56   From *Krishnamurti on Education*

57   Saanen, 28 July 1974

58   Saanen, 24 July 1975

62   Saanen, 13 July 1976

64   Madras, 31 December 1977

67   Madras, 7 January 1978

73   Ojai, 15 May 1980

77   Discussion with David Bohm, Brockwood Park,
        14 September 1980

94   Ojai, 3 May 1981

103   Rajghat, 25 November 1981

108   20 June 1983: From *The Future of Humanity*

131   Saanen, 25 July 1983

137   Brockwood Park, 30 August 1983: From *The World
        of Peace*

138   Brockwood Park, 25 August 1984

140   Madras, 2 January 1983: From *Mind Without Measure*

142   Sources and Acknowledgments

Foreword

JIDDU KRISHNAMURTI WAS born in India in 1895 and, at the age of thirteen, was taken up by the Theosophical Society, which considered him to be the vehicle for the "world teacher" whose advent it had been proclaiming. Krishnamurti was soon to emerge as a powerful, uncompromising, and unclassifiable teacher, whose talks and writings were not linked to any specific religion and were of neither the East nor the West but for the whole world. Firmly repudiating the messianic image, in 1929 he dramatically dissolved the large and monied organization that had been built around him and declared truth to be "a pathless land," which could not be approached by any formalized religion, philosophy, or sect.

For the rest of his life Krishnamurti insistently rejected the guru status that others tried to foist upon him. He continued to attract large audiences throughout the world but claimed no authority, wanted no disciples, and spoke always as one individual to another. At the core of his teaching was the realization that fundamental changes in society can be brought about only by a transformation of individual consciousness. The need for self-knowledge and understanding of the restrictive, separative influences of religious and nationalistic conditionings was constantly stressed. Krishnamurti pointed always to the urgent need for openness, for that "vast space in the brain in which there is unimaginable energy." This seems to have been the wellspring of his own creativity and the key to his catalytic impact on such a wide variety of people.

He continued to speak all over the world until he died in 1986 at the age of ninety. His talks and dialogues, journals and letters have been preserved in over sixty books and hundreds of recordings. From that vast body of teachings this series of theme books has been compiled. Each book focuses on an issue that has particular relevance to and urgency in our daily lives.

Seattle, 23 July 1950

THOUGHT IS NEVER new, but relationship is always new; and thought approaches this thing that is vital, real, new, with the background of the old. That is, thought tries to understand relationship according to the memories, patterns, and conditioning of the old— and hence there is conflict. Before we can understand relationship, we must understand the background of the thinker, which is to be aware of the whole process of thought without choice; that is, we must be capable of seeing things as they are without translating them according to our memories, our preconceived ideas, which are the outcome of past conditioning.

SO THINKING IS the response of the background, of the past, of accumulated experience; it is the response of memory at different levels, both individual and collective, particular and racial, conscious and unconscious. All that is our process of thinking. Therefore our thinking can never be new. There can be no 'new' idea because thinking can never renew itself; thinking can never be fresh because it is always the response of the background—our conditioning, our traditions, our experiences, our collective and personal accumulations. So when we look to thought as a means of discovering the new, we see the utter futility of it. Thought can only discover its own projection, it cannot discover anything new;

thought can only recognize that which it has experienced, it cannot recognize that which it has not experienced.

This is not something metaphysical, complicated, or abstract. If you will look at it a little more closely, you will see that as long as the 'I'—the entity who is made up of all these memories—is experiencing, there can never be the discovery of the new. Thought, which is the 'I', can never experience God, because God or reality is the unknown, the unimaginable, the unformulated; it has no label, no word. The word *God* is not God. So thought can never experience the new, the unknowable; it can only experience the known; it can function only within the field of the known, it cannot function beyond it. The moment there is thought about the unknown, the mind is agitated; it is always seeking to bring the unknown into the known. But the unknown can never be brought into the known, and hence the conflict between the known and the unknown.

London, 7 April 1952

WHAT IS THINKING? When we say 'l think', what do we mean by that? When are we conscious of this process of thinking? Surely, we are aware of it when there is a problem, when we are challenged, when we are asked a question, when there is friction. We are aware of it as a self-conscious process. Please do not listen to me as a lecturer holding forth; you and I are examining our own ways of thought, which we use as an instrument in our daily life. So I hope you are observing your own thinking, not merely listening to me— that is no good. We shall arrive nowhere if you are only listening to me and not observing your own process of thinking, if you are not aware of your own thought and observing the way it arises, how it comes into being. That is what we are trying to do, you and I—to see what this process of thinking is.

Surely, thinking is a reaction. If I ask you a question, to that you respond—you respond according to your memory, to your prejudices, to your upbringing, to the climate, to the whole background of your conditioning; and according to that you reply, according to that you think. If you are a Christian, a Communist, a Hindu, or what you will—that background responds—and it is this conditioning that obviously creates the problem. The centre of this background is the 'me' in the process of action. So long as that background is not understood, so long as that thought process, that self which creates the problem, is not understood and put an end to, we are bound to have conflict, within and without, in thought, in emotion, in action. No solution of any kind, however clever, however well thought out, can ever put an end to the conflict between man and man, between you and me. And realizing this, being aware of how thought springs up and from what source, then we ask, 'Can thought ever come to an end?'

That is one of the problems, is it not? Can thought resolve our problems? By thinking over the problem, have you resolved it? Any kind of problem—economic, social, religious—has it ever been really solved by thinking? In your daily life, the more you think about a problem, the more complex, the more irresolute, the more uncertain it becomes. Is that not so in our actual, daily life? You may, in thinking out certain facets of the problem, see more clearly another person's point of view, but thought cannot see the completeness and fullness of the problem, it can only see partially, and a partial answer is not a complete answer; therefore it is not a solution.

The more we think over a problem, the more we investigate, analyse, and discuss it, the more complex it becomes. So is it possible to look at the problem comprehensively, wholly? And how is this possible? That, it seems to me, is our major difficulty. For our problems are being multiplied—there is imminent danger of war, there is every kind of disturbance in our relationships—and how can we understand all that comprehensively, as a whole? Obviously, it can be solved only when we can look at it as a whole—not in compartments, not divided. And when is that possible? Surely, it is only possible when the process of thinking which has its source in the 'me', the self, in the background of tradition, of conditioning, of prejudice, of hope, of despair—has come to an end. So can we understand this self, not by analysing, but by seeing the thing as it is, being aware of it as a fact and not as a theory?—not seeking to dissolve the self in order to achieve a result, but seeing the activity of the self, the 'me', constantly in action. Can we look at it, without any movement to destroy or to encourage? That is the problem, is it not? If, in each one of us, the centre of the 'me' is non-existent, with its desire for power, position, authority, continuance, self-preservation, surely our problems will come to an end!

The self is a problem that thought cannot resolve. There must be an awareness which is not of thought. To be aware, without condemnation or justification, of the activities of the self—just to be aware—is sufficient. Because if you are aware in order to find out how to resolve the problem, in order to transform it, in order to pro-duce a result, then it is still within the field of the self, of the 'me'. So long as we are seeking a result, whether through analysis, through awareness, through constant examination of every thought, we are still within the field of thought, which is within the field of the 'me', of the 'I', of the ego.

Rajghat, 23 January 1955

Questioner: In giving talks, your ideas are born of your thinking. As you say that all thinking is conditioned, are not your ideas also conditioned?

Krishnamurti: Obviously, thinking is conditioned. Thinking is the response of memory, and memory is the result of previous knowledge and experience, which is conditioning. So all thinking is conditioned. And the questioner asks, 'Since all thinking is conditioned, is not what you are saying also conditioned?' It is really quite an interesting question, is it not?

To speak certain words, there must be memory, obviously. To communicate, you and I must know English, Hindi, or some other language. The knowing of a language is memory. That is one thing. Now, is the mind of the speaker, myself, merely using words to communicate, or is the mind in a movement of recollection? Is there memory, not merely of words, but also of some other process, and is the mind using words to communicate that other process? It is really a very interesting problem if you follow it through.

You see, the lecturer has his store of information, of knowledge, and he deals it out; that is, he remembers. He has accumulated, read, gathered; he has formed certain opinions according to his conditioning, his prejudices, and he then uses language to communicate. We all know this ordinary process. Now, is that taking place here? That is what the questioner wants to know. The questioner says, in effect, 'If you are merely remembering your experiences, your states, and communicating that memory, then what you say is conditioned'—which is true.

Please, this is very interesting because it is a revelation of the process of the mind. If you observe your own mind, you will see what I am talking about. Mind is the residue of memory, of experience, of knowledge, and from that residue it speaks; there is the background, and from that background it communicates. The questioner wants to know whether the speaker has that background and is therefore merely repeating, or whether he is speaking without the memory of the previous experience and is therefore experiencing as he is talking. You see, you are not observing your own mind. To investigate the process of thought is a delicate matter, it is like watching a living thing under a microscope. If you are not watching your own mind, you are like an outside observer watching some players in a field. But if we are all watching our own minds, then it will have tremendous significance.

If the mind is communicating through words a remembered experience, then such remembered experience is conditioned, obviously; it is not a living, moving thing. Being remembered, it is of the past. All knowledge is of the past, is it not? Knowledge can never be of the now, it is always receding into the past. Now, the questioner wants to know if the speaker is merely drawing from the well of knowledge and dealing it out. If he is, then what he communicates is conditioned because all knowledge is of the past. Knowledge is static; you may add more to it, but it is a dead thing.

So instead of communicating the past, is it possible to communicate experiencing, living? Surely, it is possible to be in a state of direct experiencing without a conditioned reaction to the experiencing, and to use words to communicate not the past, but the living thing which is being directly experienced.

When you say to somebody, 'I love you', are you communicating a remembered experience? You have used the accustomed words, 'I love you'; but is the communication a thing you have remembered, or is it something real which you immediately communicate? Which means, really, can the mind cease to be the mechanism of accumulation, storing up and therefore repeating what it has learned?

Q: I am terrified of death. Can I be unafraid of inevitable annihilation?

K: Why do you take it for granted that death is either annihilation or continuity? Either conclusion is the outcome of a conditioned desire, is it not? A man who is miserable, unhappy, frustrated, will say: 'Thank God, it is soon going to be all over, I won't have to worry any more'. He hopes for total annihilation. But the man who says, 'I have not quite finished, I want more', will hope for continuity.

Now, why does the mind assume anything with regard to death? We shall presently go into the question of why the mind is afraid of death, but first let us free the mind of any conclusion about death, because only then can you understand what death is, obviously. If you believe in reincarnation, which is a hope, a form of continuity, then you will never understand what death is, any more than you will if you are a materialist, a Communist, and believe in total annihilation. To understand what death is, the mind must be free of both the belief in continuity and the belief in annihilation. This is not a trick answer. If you want to understand something, you must not come to it having already made up your mind. If you want to know what God is, you must not have a belief about God, you must push all that away and look. If one wants to know what death is, the mind must be free of all conclusions for or against. So can your mind be free of conclusions? And if your mind is free of conclusions, is there fear? Surely, it is the conclusions that are making you afraid, and therefore there is the inventing of philosophies.

I would like to have a few more lives to finish my work, to make myself perfect, and therefore I take hope in the philosophy of reincarnation, I say, 'Yes, I shall be reborn, I shall have another opportunity', and so on. So, in my desire for continuity, I create a philosophy or accept a belief which becomes the system in which the mind is caught. And if I don't want to continue because life for me is too painful, then I look to a philosophy that assures me of annihilation. This is a simple, obvious fact.

Now, if the mind is free of both, then what is the state of the mind with regard to the fact which we call death? If the mind has no conclusions, is there death? We know that machinery wears out in use. The organism of X may last a hundred years, but it wears out. That is not what we are concerned with. But inwardly, psychologically, we want the 'I' to continue; and the 'I' is made up of conclusions, is it not? The mind has got a series of hopes, determinations, wishes, conclusions—'I have arrived', 'I want to go on writing', 'I want to find happiness'—and it wants these conclusions to continue, therefore it is afraid of their coming to an end. But if the mind has no conclusions, if it does not say, 'I am somebody', 'I want my name and my property to continue', 'I want to fulfil myself through my son', and so on, which are all desires, conclusions, then is not the mind itself in a state of constant dying? And to such a mind, is there death?

Don't agree. This is not a matter of agreement, nor is it mere logic. It is an actual experience. When your wife, your husband, your sister dies, or when you lose property, you will soon find out how you are clinging to the known. But when the mind is free of the known, then is not the mind itself the unknown? After all, what we are afraid of is leaving the known, the known being the things that we have concluded, judged, compared, accumulated. I know my wife, my house, my family, my name, I have cultivated certain thoughts, experiences, virtues, and I am afraid to let all that go. So, as long as the mind has any form of conclusion, as long as it is caught in a system, a concept, a formula, it can never know what is true. A believing mind is a conditioned mind, and whether it believes in continuity or annihilation, it can never find out what death is. And it is only now, while you are living, not when you are unconscious, dying, that you can find out the truth of that extraordinary thing called death.

Rajghat, 6 February 1955

IT IS VERY important to understand the whole process of our thinking, and the understanding of that process does not come through isolation. There is no such thing as living in isolation. The understanding of the process of our thinking comes when we observe ourselves in daily relationship, our attitudes, our beliefs, the way we talk, the way we regard people, the way we treat our husbands, our wives, our children. Relationship is the mirror in which the ways of our thinking are revealed. In the facts of relationship lies truth, not away from relationship. There is obviously no such thing as living in isolation. We may carefully cut off various forms of physical relationship, but the mind is still related. The very existence of the mind implies relationship, and self-knowledge lies through seeing the facts of relationship as they are without inventing, condemning, or justifying. In relationship the mind has certain evaluations, judgments, comparisons; it reacts to challenge according to various forms of memory, and this reaction is called thinking. If the mind can just be aware of this whole process, you will find that thought comes to a standstill. Then the mind is very quiet, very still, without incentive, without movement in any direction, and in that stillness reality comes into being.

Ojai, 21 August 1955

Questioner: The function of the mind is to think. I have spent a great many years thinking about the things we all know—business, science, philosophy, psychology, the arts, and so on—and now I think a great deal about God. From studying the evidence of many mystics and other religious writers, I am convinced that God exists, and I am able to contribute my own thoughts on the subject. What is wrong with this? Does not thinking about God help to bring about the realization of God?

Krishnamurti: Can you think about God? And can you be convinced about the existence of God because you have read all the evidence? The atheist also has his evidence; he has probably studied as much as you, and he says there is no God. You believe that there is God, and he believes that there is not; both of you have beliefs, both of you spend your time thinking about God. But before you think about something which you do not know, you must find out what thinking is, must you not? How can you think about something which you do not know? You may have read the Bible, the Bhagavad Gita, or other books in which various erudite scholars have skilfully described what God is, asserting this and contradicting that; but as long as you do not know the process of your own thinking, what you think about God may be stupid and petty, and generally it is. You may collect a lot of evidence for the existence of God and write very clever articles about it; but surely the first question is: how do you know what you think is true? And can thinking ever bring about the experience of that which is unknowable? Which doesn't mean that you must emotionally, sentimentally, accept some rubbish about God.

So is it not important to find out whether your mind is conditioned, rather than to seek that which is unconditioned? Surely, if your mind is conditioned, which it is, however much it may inquire into the reality of God, it can only gather knowledge or information according to its conditioning. So your thinking about God is an utter waste of time, it is a speculation that has no value. It is like my sitting in this grove and wishing to be on the top of that mountain. If I really want to find out what is on the top of the mountain and beyond, I must go to it. It is no good my sitting here speculating, building temples, churches, and getting excited about them. What I have to do is to stand up, walk, struggle, push, get there and find out; but as most of us are unwilling to do that, we are satisfied to sit here and speculate about something which we do not know. And I say such speculation is a hindrance, it is a deterioration of the mind, it has no value at all; it only brings more confusion, more sorrow, to man.

So God is something that cannot be talked about, that cannot be described, that cannot be put into words, because it must ever remain the unknown. The moment the recognizing process takes place, you are back in the field of memory. Say, for instance, you have a momentary experience of something extraordinary. At that precise moment, there is no thinker who says, 'I must remember it'; there is only the state of experiencing. But when that moment goes by, the process of recognition comes into being. The mind says, 'I have had a marvellous experience and I wish I could have more of it', so the struggle of the 'more' begins. The acquisitive instinct, the possessive pursuit of the 'more', comes into being for various reasons—because it gives you pleasure, prestige, knowledge, you become an authority, and all the rest of that nonsense.

The mind pursues that which it has experienced; but that which it has experienced is already over, dead, gone, and to discover that *which is*, the mind must die to that which it has experienced. This is not something that can be cultivated day after day, that can be gathered, accumulated, held, and then talked and written about. All that we can do is to see that the mind is conditioned and, through self-knowledge, to understand the process of our own thinking. I must know myself, not as I would ideologically like to be, but as I actually am, however ugly or beautiful, however jealous, envious, acquisitive. But it is very difficult just to see what one is without wishing to change it, and that very desire to change it is another form of conditioning; and so we go on, moving from conditioning to conditioning, never experiencing something beyond that which is limited.

Q: I have listened to you for many years, and I have become quite good at watching my own thoughts and being aware of everything I do. But I have never touched the deep waters or experienced the transformation of which you speak. Why?

K: I think it is fairly clear why none of us do experience something beyond the mere watching. There may be rare moments of an emotional state in which we see, as it were, the clarity of the sky between clouds, but I do not mean anything of that kind. All such experiences are temporary and have very little significance. The questioner wants to know why, after these many years of watching, he hasn't found the deep waters. Why should he find them? Do you understand? You think that by watching your own thoughts you are going to get a reward—if you do *this*, you will get *that*. You are really not watching at all, because your mind is concerned with gaining a reward. You think that by watching, by being aware, you will be more loving, you will suffer less, be less irritable, get something beyond; so your watching is a process of buying. With this *coin* you are buying *that*, which means that your watching is a process of choice;

therefore it isn't watching, it isn't attention. To watch is to observe without choice, to see yourself as you are without any movement of desire to change, which is an extremely arduous thing to do; but that doesn't mean that you are going to remain in your present state. You do not know what will happen if you see yourself as you are without wishing to bring about a change in that which you see.

I am going to take an example and work it out, and you will see. Let us say I am violent, as most people are. Our whole culture is violent, but I won't enter into the anatomy of violence now, because that is not the problem we are considering. I am violent, and I realize that I am violent. What happens? My immediate response is that I must do something about it, is it not? I say I must become non-violent. That is what every religious teacher has told us for centuries—that if one is violent, one must become non-violent. So I practise, I do all the ideological things. But now I see how absurd that is, because the entity who observes violence and wishes to change it into non-violence is still violent. So I am concerned, not with the expression of that entity, but with the entity himself.

Now, what is that entity who says, 'I must not be violent'? Is that entity different from the violence he has observed? Are they two different states? Surely, the violence and the entity who says, 'I must change violence into non-violence' are both the same. To recognize that fact is to put an end to all conflict, is it not? There is no longer the conflict of trying to change, because I see that the very movement of the mind not to be violent is itself the outcome of violence.

So the questioner wants to know why it is that he cannot go beyond all these superficial wrangles of the mind. For the simple reason that, consciously or unconsciously, the mind is always seeking something, and that very search brings violence, competition, the sense of utter dissatisfaction. It is only when the mind is completely still that there is a possibility of touching the deep waters.

Rajghat, 25 December 1955

Questioner: The question is: Where does thinking end and meditation begin?

Krishnamurti: All right, sir. Where does thinking end? Wait a minute. I am inquiring into what is thinking, and I say this very inquiry itself is meditation. It is not that there is first the ending of thinking, and then meditation begins. Please go with me, step by step. If I can find out what thinking is, then I will never ask how to meditate, because in the very process of finding out what thinking is, there is meditation. But this means that I must give complete attention to the problem, and not merely concentrate on it, which is a form of distraction.

In trying to find out what thinking is, I must give complete attention, in which there can be no effort, no friction; because in effort, friction, there is distraction. If I am really intent on finding out what thinking is, *that very question* brings an attention in which there is no deviation, no conflict, no feeling that I must pay attention.

Bombay, 28 February 1965

PLEASE LISTEN TO this. Do it, as I am talking. Do not think about doing it, but actually do it now. That is, be aware of the trees, the palm tree, the sky; hear the crows cawing; see the light on the leaf, the colour of the sari, the face, then move inwardly. You can observe, you can be aware choicelessly of outward things. It is very easy. But to move inwardly and to be aware without condemnation, without justification, without comparison, is more difficult. Just be aware of what is taking place inside you—your beliefs, your fears, your dogmas, your hopes, your frustrations, your ambitions, and all the rest of the things. Then the unfolding of the conscious and the unconscious begins. You have not to do a thing.

Just be aware; that is all you have to do, without condemning, without forcing, without trying to change what you are aware of. Then you will see that it is like a tide that is coming in. You cannot prevent the tide from coming in; build a wall, or do what you will, it will come with tremendous energy. In the same way, if you are aware choicelessly, the whole field of consciousness begins to unfold. And as it unfolds, you have to follow: and the following becomes extraordinarily difficult—following in the sense to follow the movement of every thought, of every feeling, of every secret desire. It becomes difficult the moment you resist, the moment you say, 'That is ugly', 'This is good', 'That is bad', 'This I will keep', 'That I will not keep'.

So you begin with the outer and move inwardly. Then you will find, when you move inwardly, that the inward and the outward are not two different things, that the outward awareness is not different from the inward awareness, and that they are both the same. Then you will see that you are living in the past; there is never a moment of actual living, when neither the past nor the future exists—which is the actual moment. You will find that you are always living in the past—what you felt; what you were; how clever, how good, how bad—in the memories. That is memory. So you have to understand memory, not deny it, not suppress it, not escape. If a man has taken a vow of celibacy and is holding on to that memory, when he moves out of that memory, he feels guilty; and that smothers his life.

So you begin to watch everything, and therefore you become very sensitive. Therefore by listening—by seeing not only the outward world, the outward gesture, but also the inward mind that looks and therefore feels—when you are so aware choicelessly, then there is no effort. It is very important to understand this.

From *The Only Revolution*

IS SEX THE product of thought? Is sex—the pleasure, the delight, the companionship, the tenderness involved in it—is this a remembrance strengthened by thought? In the sexual act, there is self-forgetfulness, self-abandonment, a sense of the non-existence of fear, anxiety, the worries of life. Remembering this state of tenderness and self-forgetfulness, and demanding its repetition, you chew over it, as it were, until the next occasion. Is this tenderness, or is it merely a recollection of something that is over and which, through repetition, you hope to capture again? Is not the repetition of something, however pleasurable, a destructive process?

The young man suddenly found his tongue: 'Sex is a biological urge, as you yourself have said, and if this is destructive, then isn't eating equally destructive, because that also is a biological urge?'

If one eats when one is hungry—that is one thing. If one is hungry and thought says: 'I must have the taste of this or that type of food'—then it is thought, and it is this which is the destructive repetition.

'In sex, how do you know what is the biological urge, like hunger, and what a psychological demand, like greed?' asked the young man.

Why do you divide the biological urge and the psychological demand? And there is yet another question, a different question altogether—why do you separate sex from seeing the beauty of a mountain or the loveliness of a flower? Why do you give such tremendous importance to the one and totally neglect the other?

'If sex is something quite different from love, as you seem to say, then is there any necessity at all to do anything about sex?' asked the young man.

We have never said that love and sex are two separate things. We have said that love is whole, not to be broken up, and thought, by its very nature, is fragmentary. When thought dominates, obviously there is no love. Man generally knows—perhaps only knows—the sex of thought, which is the chewing of the cud of pleasure and its repetition. Therefore we have to ask: Is there any other kind of sex which is not of thought or desire?

The *sannyasi* had listened to all this with quiet attention. Now he spoke: 'I have resisted it, I have taken a vow against it, because by tradition, by reason, I have seen that one must have energy for the religious dedicated life. But I now see that this resistance has taken a great deal of energy. I have spent more time on resisting, and wasted more energy on it, than I have ever wasted on sex itself. So what you have said—that a conflict of any kind is a waste of energy—I now understand. Conflict and struggle are far more deadening than the seeing of a woman's face, or even perhaps than sex itself'.

Is there love without desire, without pleasure? Is there sex without desire, without pleasure? Is there love which is whole, without thought entering into it? Is sex something of the past, or is it something each time new? Thought is obviously old, so we are always contrasting the old and the new. We are asking questions from the old, and we want an answer in terms of the old. So when we ask: Is there sex without the whole mechanism of thought operating and working, doesn't it mean that we have not stepped out of the old? We are so conditioned by the old that we do not feel our way into the new. We said love is whole, and always new—new not as opposed to the old, for that again is the old. Any assertion that there is sex without desire is utterly valueless, but if you have followed the whole meaning of thought, then perhaps you will come upon the other. If, however, you demand that you must have your pleasure at any price, then love will not exist.

The young man said: 'That biological urge you spoke about is precisely such a demand, for though it may be different from thought, it engenders thought'.

'Perhaps I can answer my young friend', said the *sannyasi*, 'for I have been through all this. I have trained myself for years not to look at a woman. I have ruthlessly controlled the biological demand. The biological urge does not engender thought; thought captures it, thought utilizes it, thought makes images, pictures, out of this urge—and then the urge is a slave to thought. It is thought which engenders the urge so much of the time. As I said, I am beginning to see the extraordinary nature of our own deception and dishonesty. There is a great deal of hypocrisy in us. We can never see things as they are but must create illusions about them. What you are telling us, sir, is to look at everything with clear eyes, without the memory of yesterday; you have repeated this so often in your talks. Then life does not become a problem. In my old age, I am just beginning to realize this'.

The young man looked not completely satisfied. He wanted life according to his terms, according to the formula which he had carefully built.

This is why it is very important to know oneself, not according to any formula or according to any guru. This constant choiceless awareness ends all illusions and all hypocrisy.

Now it was coming down in torrents, and the air was very still, and there was only the sound of the rain on the roof and on the leaves.

Saanen, 23 July 1970

WE HAVE ALSO to find out what is the function, what is the meaning, substance, structure of thought, because it may be thought that divides, and to find an answer through thought, through reason, it obviously must separate each problem and try to find an answer for itself. Why are we always inclined to solve our issues separately, as though they were unrelated? Some people want a physical revolution to upset the social order in order to bring about a better one, and they forget the whole psychological nature of man. So one has to ask this question—why? And in asking the question, what is the response? Is it the response of thought, or is it the response of understanding the totality of this immense, vast, structure of human life?

I want to find out why this division exists. We went into it on other occasions as the observer and the observed; let us forget that, put that aside, and approach it differently. Does thought create this division? And if we find thought does, and thought tries to find an answer to a particular problem, it remains a problem separated from other problems. Are we going together? Please don't agree with me, it is not a question of agreement, it is a question of seeing for yourself the truth or the falseness of it, not accepting— under no circumstances accept what the speaker says at any time. There is no authority when we are talking together about these matters, neither you nor the speaker have authority. We are both of us investigating, observing, looking, learning, therefore there is no question of agreement or disagreement.

One has to find out, if thought by its very nature and structure does not divide life into many, many problems; and if we try to find an answer through thought, it is still an isolated answer, and therefore breeding further confusion, further misery. So first of all, one has to find out for oneself—freely, without any bias, without any conclusion—whether thought operates in this way. Because most of us try to find an answer intellectually or emotionally, or 'intuitively'. When one uses the word *intuition*, one must be terribly careful, because in that word lies great deception. One can have intuition dictated by one's own hopes, fears, bitterness, longing, wishes; therefore one has to beware of that word and never use it. So we try to find an answer intellectually or emotionally, as though the intellect were something separate from emotion, and emotion something separate from the physical response, and so on. And as our whole education and culture are based on this intellectual approach to life, all our philosophies are based on intellectual concepts, which is rubbish. All our social structure is based on this division, as is our morality.

So if thought divides, how does it divide? Don't just play with it, actually observe it in yourself. It is much more fun, and you will see what an extraordinary thing you will discover for yourself. You will be a light to yourself, you will be an integrated human being, not looking to somebody else to tell you what to do, what to think, and how to think.

So does thought divide? And what is thought? Thought can be extraordinarily reasonable, can reason consecutively, and it needs to do so logically, objectively, sanely, because it must function perfectly, like a computer ticking over without any hindrance or conflict. Reason is necessary, sanity is part of that reasoning capacity. And what is this thinking, what is thought?

Can thought ever be new, fresh? Because every problem is new and fresh. Every human problem—not the mechanical, scientific ones—every human problem is always new. And life being new, thought tries to understand, to alter, to translate it, to do some-thing about it. So one must find out for oneself what thought is. And why does thought divide? If we really felt deeply, loved each other, not verbally but really—and that can only take place where there is no conditioning, when there is no centre as the 'me' and the 'you'—then all this division would come to an end. But thought, which is the activity of the intellect, the brain, cannot pos-sibly love. It can reason, logically, objectively, efficiently. To go to the moon, thought must have operated in the most extraordinary way, though whether going to the moon was worthwhile or not is a different matter. So thought has to be understood. And we asked whether thought can see anything new, or is there no new thought, is thought always old? And when it faces a problem of life which is always new, it cannot see the newness of it, because it tries first to translate the thing which it has observed in terms of its own condi-tioning.

So thought is necessary, it must function logically, sanely, healthily, objectively, non-emotionally, non-personally; and yet that very thought divides as the 'me' and the not 'me', and tries to solve the problem of violence by itself, as though it is unrelated to all the other problems of existence. So thought is the past. Thought is always the past; if we had no tape recorder as the brain, which has accumulated all kinds of information, experience, personal and collective, we wouldn't be able to think, to respond. Do we see that, not verbally, but *actually*? So with the past meeting the new, the new must translate in terms of the past, and therefore there is division.

You are asking why thought divides, why thought inter-prets? If thought is the result of the past, and thought is the result of yesterday, with all the information, knowledge, experience, memory, and so on, thought operates on a problem and divides that problem as though it were something separate from the rest of the other problems. Right? You are not quite sure. I am going to make you quite sure, not because I want to assert myself, which is silly, or show my argument is better than yours, which is equally silly, but we are trying to find out the truth of it, actually 'what is'. Now, leave everything aside for the moment and observe your thinking. Thought is the response of the past. If you had no past, there would be no thought, there would be a state of amnesia. The past is thought, and therefore the past will inevitably divide life as the present and the future. As long as there is the past as thought, that very past must divide life into time as the past and present and the future.

Just follow this. I am going to go into it step by step, don't jump ahead of me. I have a problem of violence, I want to understand it completely, totally, so that the mind is entirely, altogether, free from violence, and it can only understand it by understanding what is the structure of thought. It is thought that is breeding violence—'my' house, 'my' property, 'my' wife, 'my' husband, 'my' country, 'my' God, 'my' belief, which is utter nonsense. Who is doing this, creating this everlasting 'me' opposed to the rest? Who is doing it? Education, society, the establishment, the church are all doing it, because I am part of all that. And thought, which is matter, the result of memory is in the very structure and cells of the brain. Memory is the past, which is of time. And so when the brain operates, whether psychologically, socially, economically, or religiously, it must invariably operate in terms of time, the past according to its conditioning.

Thought is essential, it must function absolutely logically, completely objectively, impersonally; and yet I see how thought divides, psychologically, as well as in time. Thought must inevitably divide; look what has happened. Thought says, 'Nationalism is pretty rotten, it has led to all kinds of war and mischief, let us have brotherhood, let us all be united'. So thought founds a League of Nations or United Nations, but thought is still operating separatively and maintaining the separation: you who are an Italian, you keep your Italian sovereignty, and so on. Talk about brotherhood and yet keep separate, which is hypocrisy; that is a function of thought, to play double games with itself.

Thought is not the way out, which doesn't mean kill the mind. So what is it then that sees every problem that arises as a total problem? If one has a sexual problem, it is a total problem, related to culture, to character, to various other forms of issues of life, not by itself. Now, what is the mind that sees each problem as a whole problem, not as a fragment?

The churches, the various religions, have said, 'Seek God and everything will be solved'. As though God, according to them, is separate from life. So there has been this constant division, and I say to myself, observing this—I don't read books, but if you just observe life, you will learn more from that than from any book, both outwardly and inwardly, if you know how to look—then what is it that looks at life as a whole? Are we proceeding? What is it? Knowing the breadth, the efficiency, the vastness of thought, and knowing, observing, that thought does inevitably divide as the 'me' and the 'not me', and that the brain is the result of time, and therefore the past, and when all that structure of thought is in operation it cannot possibly see the whole, so what is it that sees life as a whole, not broken up into fragments? You have understood my question?

Questioner: There still remains a question.

Krishnamurti: We have understood but there remains a question— still there is a question. Now, who is putting that question? Thought? Inevitably. When you say you have understood but yet there remains a question, is that possible? When you have understood what thought does, completely, at every level, highest and lowest, when you see what thought does and you say, 'I have understood that very well', then when you say there is a further question, who is it that is asking that question? There is only one question, which is: this brain, the whole nervous system, the mind which covers all of that says, 'I have understood the nature of thought'. The next step is: Can this mind look at life, with all its vastness, complexity, with its apparently unending sorrow, can the mind see life as a whole? That is the only question. And thought is not putting that question; mind is putting that question because it has observed the whole structure of thought, and knows the relative value of thought, and is therefore able to say: Can the mind look with an eye that is never tainted by the past?

Now, we are going to go into that. Can the mind, the brain—which is the result of time, experience, a thousand forms of influence, accumulated knowledge, all that has been collected through time as the past—can that mind, that brain, be completely still to observe life which may have problems? This is really a very serious question, not just an entertainment. One must give one's energy, capacity, vitality, passion, *life* to this to find out, not just sit there and ask me questions. You have to give your life to find out, because that is the only response, the only way out of this terrible brutality, violence, sorrow, degradation, everything that is corrupt. Can the mind, the brain, which is itself corrupt through time, can all that be quiet so that it can see life as a whole and therefore without problems? When you see something as a whole, how can there be a problem? A problem only arises when you see life fragmentarily. Do see the beauty of that. When you see life as a whole, then there is no problem whatsoever. It is only a mind and a heart and a brain which are broken up as fragments that create problems. The centre of this fragment is the 'me', the 'me' is brought about through thought, which has no reality by itself. The 'me', 'my' house, 'my' furniture, 'my' bitterness, 'my' disappointment, 'my' desire to become somebody, the 'me' is the product of thought— 'my' sexual appetites, 'my' bitterness, 'my' anxiety, 'my' guilt—the 'me', which is the product of thought, divides. And can the mind look without the 'me'? Not being able to do this, to look at life without the 'me', that very 'me' says: 'I will dedicate myself to Jesus, to Buddha, to this, to that'—you understand? 'I will become a Communist who will be concerned with the whole of the world'. The 'me' identifying itself with what it considers to be the greater is still part of the 'me'.

Saanen, 26 July 1970

WE ARE ASKING the mind to examine itself and perceive the sequence of fear, its activities, its dangers. So we are going to examine not only physical fears, but also the very, very complex fears that lie deeply below the conscious mind. Most of us have had physical fears, either fear of past illness, with all its pain and anxiety, or we have faced physical danger. And when you face danger of a physical kind, is there fear? Please inquire, don't say, 'Yes, there is fear'—find out. In India, Africa, and wild parts of America, when you come across a bear, or a snake, or a tiger, there is immediate action. Isn't there? When you meet a snake, there is immediate action; it is not conscious, deliberate action, there is instinctive action.

Now, is that fear? Or is that intelligence? Because we are trying to find out action which is intelligence and action which is born of fear. When you meet a snake, there is an instant physical response. You run away, you sweat, you try to do something about it. That response is a conditioned response because you have been told for generations to be careful of snakes, to be careful of wild animals. It is a conditioned response, so the brain, the nerves, respond instinctively to protect themselves. Protecting oneself is a natural, intelligent response. Are you following all this? To protect the physical organism is necessary and a snake is a danger, and to respond to it protectively is an intelligent action.

Now, look at the other case, which is physical pain. You have had pain last year or yesterday, and you are afraid that it might return. The fear there is caused by thought. Thinking about something that happened a year ago or yesterday and might happen again tomorrow is fear brought about by thought. Go into it, please, we are sharing it together. Which means you are watching your own responses, what your own activities have been. There fear is the product of conscious or unconscious thought—thought being time. Not chronological time by the watch, but time as thought thinking about the thing that happened yesterday or some time ago and the fear of it happening again. So thought is time. And thought produces fear: I might die tomorrow, or something I have done in the past might be exposed; thinking about that breeds fear. Now, are you doing it? You have had pain, you have done something in the past which you don't want to have exposed, or you want to fulfil or do something in the future and you may not be able to, which is all the product of thought and time. Are you doing this? Most people are.

Now, can this movement of thought which breeds fear in time and as time, can that come to an end? You have understood my question? There is the intelligent action of protection, self-preservation, physical necessity to survive, which is a natural, intelligent response. The other, thought thinking about something and projecting the possibility of its not happening or of its happening again, breeds fear. So the question is: Can this movement of thought, so instinctual, so immediate, so insistent, so persuasive, naturally come to an end? Not through opposition! If you oppose it, it is still the product of thought, if you exercise your will to stop it, it is still the product of thought. If you say, 'I will not allow myself to think that way', who is the entity that says, 'I will not'? It is still thought because by stopping that movement, it hopes to achieve something else, which is still the product of thought. Therefore thought may project it and may not be able to achieve it, and then there is fear involved in it.

So we are asking whether thought which has produced this psychological fear—not just one fear, but many, many fears—whether that whole activity can naturally, easily, effortlessly, come to an end. Because if you make an effort it is still thought and therefore productive of fear, and still caught within the field of time. So one has to find a way, understand, or learn about a way whereby thought will naturally come to an end, and cease to create fear. Are we communicating with each other? I don't know! Verbally, perhaps, you have seen the idea clearly, the division clearly, that's not it. We are not talking merely verbally, but about your fear, your daily life; that's what we are talking about—your life, not the description of your life. Because the description is not the described, the explanation is not the explained. The word is not the thing. But it is your life, your fear; and it is not being exposed by the speaker; by listening *you* have learned to expose what fear is and how thought creates fear.

So we are asking whether thought, the activity of thought, which engenders, breeds, sustains, and nourishes fear, can naturally, happily, easily, come to an end, without any determination, without any resistance, without any activity of the will.

Now, before we can complete that question by discovering the true answer, we also have to inquire into the pursuit, conscious or unconscious, of pleasure, because it is thought again that sustains pleasure. You had a lovely moment when you looked at the sunset yesterday; you said, 'What a marvellous sunset', you took great delight in it. Then thought steps in and says, 'How nice it was, I would like to have that experience repeated again tomorrow'—whether it is a sunset, or somebody who flatters you, whether it is a sexual experience, or some other pleasure you have achieved, you want to go on experiencing. Pleasure isn't merely just sexual pleasure; there is pleasure derived through achievement, through being somebody, the pleasure of success, the pleasure of fulfilment, the pleasure of what you are going to do tomorrow, the pleasure of something which you have experienced artistically, or in different ways, and wanting that repeated. All that is pleasure. And our social morality is based on pleasure, isn't it? Social morality is based on pleasure, and therefore it is no morality at all, it is immoral. You are going to find that out—which doesn't mean by revolting against the social morality, you are going to become very moral, doing what you like, sleeping with whom you like. Play with all this, you will find out.

So if you are going to understand and be free of fear, one must also understand pleasure because they are interrelated. Which doesn't mean you must give up pleasure. You know all the organized religions—and they have been the bane of civilization—have said you must have no pleasure, no sex. God won't allow you, you must approach God as a tortured human being. So you mustn't look at a woman, you mustn't look at a tree, you mustn't look at the beauty of the sky, you mustn't look at the lovely lines of a hill, which might remind you of sex and women. You must not have pleasure, which means you must not have desire. So pick up your Bible when the desire arises, lose yourself in that, or the Gita, or repeat some words, all that nonsense.

So to understand fear one must also examine the nature of pleasure. If you don't have pleasure tomorrow, you are going to be afraid, to be frustrated. You have had pleasure yesterday, sexually or otherwise, and if you cannot have it tomorrow, you get angry, upset, hysterical, which is a form of fear. So fear and pleasure are two sides of the coin; you cannot be free of one and not be free of the other also. I know you want to have pleasure all your life *and* be free of fear, that's all you are concerned about. But you don't see that if you have no pleasure tomorrow, you feel frustrated, unfulfilled, you feel angry, anxious, guilty, and all the psychological miseries arise. So you have to look at both.

In understanding pleasure you have also to understand what joy is. Is pleasure joy, is pleasure enjoyment, is pleasure something totally different from the full delight of existence? We are going to find out all this. First we are asking whether thought with all its activities, which breeds fear and sustains fear, conscious or unconscious, whether that can come naturally to an end, without effort. There are conscious fears, as well as unconscious fears of which you are not aware. The fears of which one is not aware play a much greater part in one's life than the fears one is aware of. Now, how are you going to uncover the unconscious fears? How are you going to expose them to the light? By analysis? Who is then to analyse? If you say, 'I will analyse my fears', who is the analyser? Part of the fragment of fear. Therefore analysis of one's own fears has no value at all. I don't know if you see this. If you go to an analyst to have your fears analysed, the analyst is also like you, conditioned by the specialist, by Freud, Jung, and Adler, and X Y Z. He analyses according to his conditioning. Right? Therefore it doesn't help you to be free of fear. As we said, all analysis is a negation of action.

So CAN YOU observe during the day the whole movement of your activities, thoughts, feelings, without interpretation, just watching? Then you will see dreams have very little meaning, you will hardly ever dream. If during the daytime you are awake, not half asleep— if you are not caught by your beliefs, by your prejudices, by your absurd little vanities and pride, your petty little knowledge, but merely observe the whole movement of your conscious and unconscious mind in action—you will see not only that there will be an end to dreams, but also that thought begins to subside, no longer seeking or sustaining pleasure or avoiding fear.

HASN'T YOUR MIND become a little more sensitive? Before you just walked, carrying this burden of fear and pleasure. By learning the weight of the burden, haven't you put it aside, haven't you dropped it, and therefore you are walking very carefully? If you have really followed this, listened to it, shared it together, learned together, your mind by observing—not through determination, not through effort, but merely observing—has become sensitive and therefore very intelligent. Please, don't agree; if it is not sensitive, it is not sensitive—don't play a game.

So the next time fear arises, as it will, intelligence will respond to it not in terms of pleasure, of suppressing or escaping. This intelligent, sensitive mind, which has come about by examining, learning, looking at this burden, has put it aside and has therefore become astonishingly alive, sensitive. Then it can ask quite a different question, which is: If pleasure is not the way of life, as it has been for most of us, then is life barren? Is life dry? Or what is the difference between pleasure and joy? Does it mean I can never enjoy life? Please don't agree, find out. You enjoyed life before in terms of pleasure and fear. The instant pleasure, sex, drink, eating food, killing an animal, stuffing yourself with meat, and all the rest of it. The instant pleasure. That's been your way of life. And you suddenly discover by examining, looking, that pleasure isn't the way at all because it leads to fear, to frustration, to misery, to sorrow, to great sociological as well as personal disturbances, and so on. So now you ask quite a different question. You ask: What is joy?

Is there joy which is untouched by thought and pleasure? Because if it is touched by thought, it again becomes pleasure, and therefore fear. So is there a way of living daily, having understood pleasure and fear, a way of life which is joyous, which is enjoyment, not the carrying over of pleasure and fear from day to day?

Do you know what enjoyment is? To look at those mountains, the beauty of the valley, the light on the hills, and the trees, and the flowing river, to enjoy it. And when do you enjoy it? When the mind, when thought, is not using that as a means of pleasure. You can look at that mountain, or the face of a woman or a man, the lines of a valley, the movement of a tree, and take tremendous delight in it. When you have done that it is finished; but if you carry it over, then pain and pleasure begin. Can you look and finish with it? Be careful of this, be very watchful of this. That is, can you look at that mountain—not be absorbed by its beauty like a child with a toy being absorbed by the toy and returning to its mischief again— but look at that beauty and the very look is enough, the delight in it, and not carry it over, wishing for it tomorrow. Which means—see the danger—you can have some great pleasure and *say* it is over. But is it over? Is not the mind consciously or unconsciously building, chewing over it, thinking about it, wishing it to happen again soon? Thought has nothing whatsoever to do with joy. Please, all this is a tremendous discovery for yourself, not just being told about it. So there is a vast difference between delight, enjoyment, joy, bliss, and pleasure.

❖

So you can observe all this and find out the beauty of living, and there *is* such beauty, in which there is no effort but living with great ecstasy, in which pleasure and thought and fear don't enter at all.

Saanen, 18 July 1972

It is astonishingly beautiful and interesting, how thought is absent when you have an insight. Thought cannot have an insight. It is only when the mind is not operating mechanically in the structure of thought that you have an insight. Having had an insight, thought draws a conclusion from that insight. And then thought acts and thought is mechanical. So I have to find out whether having an insight into myself, which means into the world, and not drawing a conclusion from it is possible. If I draw a conclusion, I act on an idea, on an image, on a symbol, which is the structure of thought, and so I am constantly preventing myself from having insight, from understanding things as they are. So I have to go into this whole question of why thought interferes and draws a conclusion when there is a perception.

I perceive something to be true, I perceive that to control oneself—listen to this carefully—to control oneself brings about a division in myself, the controller and the controlled, and therefore conflict. I have an insight into that, that is the truth, but my whole thinking process is conditioned by the idea that I must control; my education, my religion, the society in which I live, the family structure, everything says to me 'control', which is the conclusion which has been handed down to me, the conclusion which I have also acquired, and I act according to that conclusion, which is mechanical. And therefore I live in constant strife. Now, I have an insight into this whole problem of control. So I have an insight which came into being when the mind was free to observe, unconditioned, but this whole structure of conditioning still remains. So there is now a mind that says, 'By Jove, I have seen this thing very clearly, but I am also caught in the habit of control'. So there is a battle—the one is mechanical, the other is non-mechanical. Now, why does thought cling to the whole structure of control? Because thought has brought about this idea of control.

What does it mean to control? It implies suppression, division in oneself, which means one part, one segment of me, says, 'I must control the other segments'. That division is created by thought. Thought says, 'I must control myself because otherwise I will not adapt myself to the environment, to what people say, and so on and so on, therefore I must control'. So thought, being the response of memory—and memory is the past, memory is experience, knowledge, which are all mechanical—has immense power. So there is constant battle between perception, insight, and conditioning.

Now, what is the mind to do? This is our problem. You see something new but the old is still there—the old habits, the old ideas, the beliefs, all that is tremendously weighting. Now, how is the mind to sustain an insight without at any time having a conclusion? Because if I have a conclusion, it is mechanical, the result of thought, the result of memory. From memory there is a reaction as thought. Then it becomes mechanical, then it becomes old. Please experiment with me.

There is insight, seeing something totally new, clear, beautiful, and there is the past with all the memories, experience, knowledge, and from that arises thought that is cautious, watching, afraid, wondering how to bring the new into the old. Now, when you see this clearly, what takes place? We are the result of the past; and though the younger generation may try to break away from it and think they are free to create a new world, they are not free from the past. They are reacting to the past and therefore continuing with the past.

So I see this. I see what thought has done, and also there is a clear perception that insight exists only when there is the absence of thought. Now, how do you solve this problem? I do not know if you have thought about it, and perhaps you are looking at it for the first time. How do you, how does the mind, respond to this?

Let me put the question differently. Mind must have knowledge: I must know where I live. It must know the language it speaks. It must exercise thought—thought which is the response of memory, experience, knowledge, which is the past. It must operate; otherwise, if I could not think clearly, there would be no communication between you and me. So I see knowledge is necessary to function in the mechanical world. Going from here to the place where I live, speaking a language, acting from knowledge, acting from all kinds of experience, is mechanical. And that mechanical process must, to a certain extent, continue. That is my insight. Have you got it? So there is no contradiction between knowledge and freedom from knowledge when there is an insight.

The insight I have now is that knowledge is necessary, and also that there is that insight which comes when there is the absence of thought. So there is perception, insight all the time, and no contradiction.

See the difficulty of putting into words what I want to convey. I want to convey to you that a mind that is constantly operating upon a conclusion inevitably becomes mechanical, and being mechanical it must escape into some kind of illusion, some kind of mythology, some kind of religious circus. And you have an insight into that. You say, 'By Jove, how true that is'. Now, if you draw a conclusion from that insight, you have moved to a different place but it is still mechanical. So when you have constant insight without conclusion, that state of mind is creative—not the mind that is in conflict and through conflict produces pictures, books. That mind can never be creative. Now, if you see that, that is an insight, isn't it?

You know, in literature, in the world of art, people say someone is a great artist, a great creative writer. Now, if you look behind the literature at the author, you will see that he is in daily conflict—with his wife, with his family, with society, he is ambitious, greedy, he wants power, position, prestige. And he has certain talents for writing. Through tensions, through conflict, he may write very good books but he is not creative in the deep sense of the word. And we are trying to see if each one of us can be creative in the deep sense of that word—not in expression, that is, in writing a book, poem, or whatever it is, but having insight and never drawing a conclusion from that insight, so that you are moving constantly from insight to insight, action to action. That is spontaneity.

Now, such a mind must obviously be alone—not in the sense of being isolated. You know the difference between isolation and being alone? I am isolated when I build a wall of resistance round myself. I resist. I resist any criticism, any new idea, I am afraid, I want to protect myself, I don't want to be hurt. And therefore that brings about in my action a self-centred activity, which is an isolating process. Is that clear? And most of us are isolating ourselves. I have been hurt and I don't want to be hurt. The memory of that hurt remains, and therefore I resist. Or I believe in Jesus or Krishna, or whatever it is, and I resist any question of doubt, anything criticizing my belief because I have taken security in my belief. That isolates. That isolation may include thousands of people, millions of people, but it is still isolation. When I say I am a Catholic or a Communist or whatever, I am isolating myself. And aloneness is entirely different, it is not the opposite of isolation but—listen to this carefully—having an insight into isolation. *That insight is aloneness.*

You know, death is the final state of complete isolation. You are leaving everything behind, all your works, your ideas; you are completely isolated through fear of that thing. And that isolation is wholly different from understanding the whole nature of death. If you have an insight into that, you are alone.

So a mind that is free has insight every minute, a mind that is free has no conclusion and is therefore non-mechanical. Such a mind is in action, non-mechanical action, because it sees the fact, has insight into everything each minute. Therefore it is constantly moving, alive. And so such a mind is always young, fresh, and incapable of being hurt, whereas the mechanical mind is capable of being hurt.

So thought, upon which all our civilizations are built, becomes mechanical, all our civilizations are mechanical. And therefore they are corrupt. Therefore to belong to any organization is to become corrupt, or to allow oneself to be corrupted. Now, that is an insight, isn't it? Now, can you move from that insight to another insight and keep moving, which is living, and therefore relationship becomes a totally different thing? Our relationships are based on conclusions, aren't they? Do watch this, please do have an insight into this, and you will see how extraordinary a change takes place in your relationships.

First of all, our relationship is mechanical, which means our relationship is based on ideas, on a conclusion, on images. I have an image about my wife, or she has an image about me—image in the sense of knowledge, a conclusion, experience—and from that conclusion, knowledge, image, she acts, and she adds to that image, conclusion, through action, as I do. So the relationship is between two conclusions. And therefore it is mechanical. You may call it love, you may sleep together, but it is mechanical. Being mechanical, then you want excitement—religious excitement, psychological excitement—and every form of entertainment, escape from this mechanical relationship. You divorce, and try to find another woman or man who will have something new, but that soon becomes mechanical.

So our relationships are based on this mechanical process. Now, if you have an insight into this, see it as it actually is—the pleasure, the so-called love, the so-called antagonism, the frustrations, the images, conclusions, that you have built about her and about yourself—if you have an insight into that, all that disappears, doesn't it? You no longer have an image, which is a conclusion. So your relationship is direct, not through an image. But our relationship is based on thought, on the intellect, which is mechanical, and that has nothing whatsoever to do with love, obviously. I may say, 'I love my wife', but it is not the actual fact. *I love the image which I have about her when she is not attacking me.* So I discover that relationship means freedom from images, conclusions, and therefore means responsibility and love. Which is not a conclusion, you understand?

So my brain is the storehouse of knowledge, various experiences, memories, hurts, images, which is thought—right? Do see this. And my brain, which is yours as well as mine, my brain is conditioned through time, through evolution, through growth. And its function is to live in complete security, naturally, otherwise it can't function. So it builds a wall round itself as belief, dogma, prestige, power, position—all that; it builds that around itself to be completely secure. Have you watched your own brain operating? Then you will find that it can function remarkably well, logically, sanely, when it is not frightened. That means when it has complete security. Now, is there complete security? So being uncertain of complete security, it then proceeds to conclude that there is security. It makes a conclusion. So conclusion becomes its security. I am frightened, I see I can only function, the brain can only function, when there is really happy, enjoyable security. But I can't enjoy it because I am frightened, I may lose my job, my wife. I am frightened—and so through fear I invest my energy in a belief, in a conclusion; *that* becomes my security. That belief, that conclusion, may be an illusion, a myth, a nonsense, but it is my security. People believe in all the business of churches; it is an absolute myth, but that is their security. So I find security in a belief, or in some neurotic behaviour— because to behave neurotically is also a form of security.

So the brain can only function freely, fully, in complete security. It must have security, whether it is real or false, illusory or non-existent, so it will invent a security. Now, I see that there is no security in belief, in a conclusion, in any person, in any social structure, in any leader, in following anybody. I see that there is no security in that. So I have security in seeing, in having insight. *There is security in insight, not in conclusion.* Have you got it? Not from me, for yourself. Have you captured it, is it real to you?

So we have this problem of a mind or brain that can only function in complete order, in complete security, in complete certainty; otherwise it gets deranged, neurotic. Therefore I see that any person, myself included, who belongs to any organization, putting his faith in an organization, his faith in a leader, acts neurotically. What is the security that a mind has when it has discarded all this? Its security is in the insight which brings intelligence. Security is intelligence. It is not knowledge, not experience, but insight into the value of knowledge that is the capacity of sustained intelligence, and in that there is security. Therefore that intelligence, that insight is never frightened.

❖

IT WOULD BE a tremendous thing if we could, all of us together, understand this one thing: the nature of awareness, nature of perception, nature of insight. Because then the mind is free to live. To *live*, not to live in conflict, in battle, in suspicion, in fear, being hurt, and all the rest of that misery.

Saanen, 20 July 1972

I THINK THE CENTRAL problem of our existence is thought, the whole machinery of thinking. Our civilization, both in the East and the West, is based on thought, on the intellect. Thought is very limited, it is measurable, and thought has done the most extraordinary things in the world—the whole technological world, going to the moon, the possibility of building houses that are comfortable for everybody. But thought has also done a great deal of mischief—all the instruments of war, the destruction of Nature, the pollution of the earth—and also, if one goes into it very deeply, it has created the so-called religions throughout the world. Thought has been responsible for the mythology of the Christians, with their Saviour, popes, priests, salvation, and all the rest of it. Also, thought has been responsible for a particular kind of culture with its technological and artistic development, and the cruelty, the brutality in relationship, the class divisions, and so on. This machinery of thought is mechanical, is a mechanistic philosophy, mechanistic physics, and thought has divided human beings as the 'me' and the 'not me', the 'we' and 'they', the Hindu, the Buddhist, the Communist, the young and the old, the hippies, non-hippies, the established order, and so on. All that structure is the result of thought. I think that is fairly clear, whether in the religious, secular, political, or national areas.

Thought has created an extraordinary world—the marvellous cities now decaying, rapid transportation. And thought has also divided human beings in their relationship. Thought, which is the response of memory, experience, knowledge, divides human beings. That is, in our relationship with each other, thought has built, through a series of incidents, activities, the image of the 'me' and the 'you'. The images that exist through constant interacting relationship. These images are mechanistic and therefore relationship becomes mechanical.

So there is not only the division brought about by thought in the outside world, but also there is division in the human being inwardly. And one sees thought is necessary, absolutely necessary, otherwise you can't go to your house, you can't write a book, you can't talk. Thinking then is the response of memory, experience, knowledge, which is the past. Thought projects the future through the present, modifying it, shaping it, designing it as the future.

So thought has a logical, efficient function, if it is not personal. There is accumulated knowledge as science and all the accumulation of ideas. Knowledge becomes important, but knowledge, the known, prevents the mind going beyond the present and the past. Thought can only function in the field of the known, though it may project the unknown according to its conditioning, to its knowledge of the known. And you observe this phenomenon right through the world—the ideal, the future, the 'what should be', what must happen according to the background, the conditioning, education, the environment. And thought is responsible also for behaviour, the vulgarity, the crudeness, the brutality, the violence in all relationships, and so on. And so thought is measurable.

The West is the explosion of the culture of the Greeks, who thought in terms of measure. For them, mathematics, logic, philosophy, were the result of measurement, which is thought. Without understanding the whole machinery of thought and its tremendous significance, and where it becomes utterly destructive, meditation has no meaning. Unless you really understand, have a deep insight into the whole machinery of thinking, you cannot possibly go beyond it. In the East, India exploded over the whole of Asia. (Not modern India, but ancient India—the modern Indians are just like you—romantic, vulgar, superstitious, frightened, grabbing money, wanting position, power, prestige, following some guru, you know all that business that goes on in the rest of the world—only they are a different colour, have a different climate, a partially different morality.) So the ancient Indians said measurement is illusion because when you can measure something, it is very limited; and if you base all your structure, all your morality, all your existence on measurement, which is thought, then you can never be free. Therefore they said, at least according to what I have observed, that the immeasurable is the real and the measurable is the unreal, which they called Maya.

But you see thought—as the intellect, the capacity to understand, to observe, to be able to think logically together, to design, to construct—thought shaped the human mind, human behaviour. In Asia they said to find the immeasurable, you must control thought, you must shape it through behaviour, through righteous conduct, through various forms of personal sacrifice, and so on. It is exactly the same thing in the West. In the West also they said control, behave, don't hurt, don't kill, but both the East and West killed, misbehaved—did everything.

We cannot possibly deny that thought is the central issue of our existence. We may imagine that we have a soul, that there is a God, that there is heaven, hell, but we invent all these things by thought; the noble qualities and the ugly existence are all the product of the machinery of thinking. So one asks oneself: If the world, the outer existence, is the result of mechanistic philosophy, mechanistic physics, what place has thought in relationship, and what place has thought in the investigation of the immeasurable, if there is the immeasurable? You must find out, and this is where we are going to share together.

I want to find out what thought is and what significance thinking has for existence. If thought is measurable and therefore very limited, can thought investigate something which is not of time, of experience, of knowledge? You understand my question? Can thought investigate the immeasurable, the unknown, the unnameable, the eternal, the everlasting—they have given it dozens of names, which is not important. For if thought cannot investigate it, then what is the mind that is capable of entering into that dimension which has no word? Right? Because the word is thought. We use a word to convey a particular idea, a particular thought, a particular feeling. So thought, which is concerned with remembering, imagining, contriving, designing, calculating, and therefore functioning from a centre, which is the accumulated knowledge as the 'me', can that thought investigate something which it cannot possibly understand? Because it can only function in the field of the known; otherwise thought is puzzled, is incapable.

So what is thinking? I want to be very clear in myself to find out what thinking is. And to discover or find out its right place. We said thinking is the response of memory, experience, knowledge stored up in the brain cells. Therefore thought is the result of development, evolution, which is time. So thought is the result of time, and it can function only within the space it creates around itself And that space is very limited, that space is the 'me' and the 'not you'. Thought, the whole machinery of thinking, has a rightful place. And thought in relationship between two human beings be-comes destructive. Do you see it? Thought, the product of knowledge, time, evolution, the result of mechanistic philosophy, science, which are all based on thought—though occasionally a new discov-ery takes place in which thought doesn't enter at all. That is, you discover something totally new, and that discovery is not the discov-ery of thought. You then translate what you have discovered in terms of thought, in terms of the known. A great scientist, though he may have immense knowledge, that knowledge is absent at the mo-ment of seeing something new. He has an insight into something to-tally new, then he translates it into the known, into words, a phrase, logical sequences. And such thinking is necessary.

So knowledge is absolutely essential. You can add to it, take away from it, but the immensity of knowledge is a human necessity. Now, is knowledge necessary in relationship between human beings? We are related to each other, we are human beings, we live on the same earth, it is our earth, not the Christian or English or Indian earth, it is our earth, the beauty of it, the marvellous riches of it, it is our earth to be lived on. And what place has thought in relationship? Relationship means to be related, relationship means to respond to each other in freedom, with its responsibility. So what place has thought in relationship? Thought, which is capable of remembering, imagining, contriving, designing, calculating: What place has it in human relationship? Has it any place at all? Please, we are inquiring into ourselves, not somewhere else mechanically.

Is thought love? Don't deny it, we are inquiring, going into it. What is our relationship when we live together in a house, husband, wife, friend, what is our relationship? Is it based on thought?—which is also feeling, the two cannot be divided. If it is based on thought, then relationship becomes mechanistic. And for most of us, that is the relationship we have with each other—mechanistic. I mean by mechanistic the image created by thought about you and about me. The images that each one creates, defends, through a number of years, or through a number of days. You have built an image about me and I have built an image about you, which is the product of thought. The image becomes the defence, the resistance, the calculation, I build a wall around myself and a wall around you, and you build a wall around yourself and a wall around me—this is called relationship, which is a fact.

So our relationship is the product of thought, calculated, remembered, imagined, contrived. And is that relationship? It is easy to say 'No, of course not'. When you put it so clearly, of course it isn't. But the fact is, it *is* our relationship. If we don't deceive ourselves, that is the fact. I don't want to be hurt, I don't mind hurting you, and so I build a resistance, and you do the same. This process of interrelationship becomes mechanistic and destructive. And being a mechanistic, destructive relationship, we try to escape from it, consciously or unconsciously.

So I discover, I have an insight, that any kind of interference of thought in relationship becomes mechanistic. I have discovered it. To me that is *an immense fact*—that when thought interferes in relationship, it is as destructive as a snake or a precipice or a dangerous animal. I see that. So what am I to do? I see thought is necessary at a certain level, and that thought in relationship is the most destructive thing. That is, you have hurt me, said things to me, flattered me, given me pleasure, sexual or otherwise, nagged me, bullied me, dominated me, brought about frustrations—those are all the images, conclusions I have about you. And when I see you, I project all that. I may try to control it, I may try to suppress it, but it is always there. So what is one to do? I see, I have an insight, into the whole machinery of thinking—the whole machinery, not in one direction, the machinery of thinking in human existence, outwardly and inwardly, it is the same movement. And if the mind is to go beyond it, beyond and above it, how is thought to be given enough scope to play without bringing about its own frustration? Come on, see the *beauty* of all this!

Because without understanding, without coming into that state of something which can never be entered into by thought, life becomes very mechanical, routine, boring, tiresome—you know what it is. And knowing that it is lonesome, dreadful, ugly, with occasional pleasure or joy, we want to escape, to run away from this horror. And therefore we imagine, create myths—and myths have a certain place. The Christian myth has held people together, the Indians have great myths, and these myths have brought about a unity; and when they go fragmentation takes place, which is going on in the world at the present time. If you really think about it very seriously, you have no myths about Jesus or Buddha, you have dropped all that.

So how is the mind to bring about a harmony in which the division between the known and freedom from the known doesn't exist? The known is knowledge, the functioning of thought, and freedom from it. The two moving together, in perfect harmony, in balance, in the beauty of movement. Have you understood this?

Have you seen the question first? And the beauty of that question? Not an integration of the two, which is impossible, because integration means putting several parts together, adding new parts, or taking away old parts; that implies an entity capable of doing this, an outsider who is the invention of thought. Like the soul, the atman in India, and so on, it is still thought. So my question is: Can they be like two rivers joining together, moving together, the known and the unknown, the freedom from the known, and a mind that has insight into a dimension in which thought doesn't happen at all?

So is this possible? Or is it merely an idea, merely a theory? Though the original dictionary meaning of *theory* is to have an insight, to have the capacity to observe instantly the truth of something, to behold. Now, that is the problem. Thought and non-thought. Thought—when I have to build a bridge, write a book, make a speech, calculate where I shall go—I use thought. And in relationship no thought at all, because that is love. Now, can the two move together all the time?

Can the two live harmoniously together, so that behaviour is not based on thought, since then it becomes mechanistic, conditioned, a relationship of images? So can there be this movement of knowledge—because it is always moving, it isn't static, you are always adding—and the movement in which thought as image-maker doesn't enter at all? If the question is clear, then you will see thought, which is still operating, says, to do that you must control. You understand? You must control thought, you must hold it and not let it interfere in relationship, you must build a wall. So thought is calculating, imagining, remembering—remembering what somebody has said about these two movements having to go together. So thought says, 'I will remember that, it is a marvellous idea'—so it stores it up as memory and, according to that memory, it is going to act. Therefore it says, 'I must control'. And all mechanistic philosophy, civilization, all religious structure is based on this—control—after you have controlled, sufficiently suppressed, then you will be free, which is sheer nonsense!

So thought begins to create a pattern of how to behave in order to have that harmony. Therefore it has *destroyed* it! Now, I have an insight. I have an insight into this question, that control is not the way—control implies suppression, an entity which controls, which is still thought as the controller, the observer, the see-er, the experiencer, the thinker. I have an insight into that. So what does the mind do?

How do you have an insight? What is insight? How does it take place? You know what I mean by insight—when you see something as the false and something as the truth, see it instantly. You do, on occasion. You see something totally and say, 'By Jove, how true that is'. Now, what is the state of mind that says, 'It is so'? —which has nothing to do with thought, which has nothing to do with logic or dialectic, which is opinion. What is the state of the mind that sees the fact instantly, and therefore the truth of it? Obviously, if the thinker is there, there is no perception. Right? If thought says, 'I will bring about an extraordinary state by suppression, control, by various forms of sacrifice, asceticism, no sex, or whatever it is'—it goes through all these phenomena, hoping to come upon the other. The other is sought because this is limited, this is tiresome, boring, mechanical, so in its desire to have more pleasure, more excitement, it will accept the other.

❖

So WE ARE now inquiring into what it is to observe without the observer. Because the observer is the past, is within the field of thought, because it is the result of knowledge, therefore experience and so on. So is there an observation without the observer, which is the past? Can I look at you, my wife, my friend, my neighbour, without the image which I have brought about through relationship? Can I look at you without all that coming into being? Is that possible? You have hurt me, you have said unpleasant things about me, you have spread scandalous rumours about me. And can I look at you without bearing all that memory? Which means, can I look at you without any interference of thought, which has remembered the insult, the hurt, or the flattery? Can I look at a tree without the knowledge of that tree? Can I listen to the sound of the river going by without naming or recognizing it—just listen to the beauty of the sound? Can you do this? You may listen to the river, you may see the mountain without any calculated design, but can you look at yourself with all your conscious or unconscious accumulations, look at yourself with eyes that have never been touched by the past? Have you tried any of this? Sorry, I shouldn't have said 'tried'. To try is wrong. Have you *done* it? Looked at your wife, your girl-friend, boyfriend, or whatever it is, without a single memory of the past? Then you discover that thought is repetitive, mechanical, and relationship is not, so you discover love is not the product of thought. Therefore there is no such thing as divine love and human love, there is only love.

❖

WITHOUT THE WORD is there thought? Or is the mind such a slave to words that it cannot see the movement of thought without the word? That is: Can I, can the mind, observe 'me', the whole content of 'me', without the word? Observe what I am without as-sociation—the association is the word, the memory, the remem-brance—therefore there is a learning about myself without any remembrance, without the accumulated knowledge as experience of anger, jealousy, antagonism, or desire for power. So can I look at myself—not I—can the mind look at itself without the movement of the word, because the word is the thinker, the word is the observer?

Now, to look so clearly, the mind must be astonishingly free from any attachment, whether to a conclusion, which is an image, or to an idea, which is the product of thought—the idea being put together by words, phrases, concepts—or attachment to any principle, to any movement of fear and pleasure. Such percep-tion is in itself the highest form of discipline—discipline in the sense of learning, not conforming.

We began with inquiring into and therefore sharing to-gether the question: What is the place of thought in existence? For our life as it is now, all our existence is based on thought; thought may imagine existence is not based on it, that it is based on something spiritual, but that is still the product of thought. Our gods, our saviours, our masters, our gurus, are the product of thought. And what place has thought in life, in existence? It has its place logically, sanely, effectively, when knowledge functions without the interference of the 'me' who is using knowledge, the 'me' who says, 'I am a better scientist than that person', 'I am a better guru than that guru'. So knowledge when used without the 'me', which is the product of thought, which creates the division between 'me' and 'you', is the most extraordinary thing because that will bring about a better world, a better structure of the world, a better society. We have enough knowledge to bring about a happy world, where we can all have food, clothing, shelter, vocation, no ghettos, but that is denied because thought has separated itself as the 'me' and the 'you', my country and your country, my beastly god and your beastly god, and we are at war with each other.

So thought as memory, remembrance, imagination, design has a logical, healthy place, but it can never come into relationship. If you see that—not logically, not verbally, not with the sense 'I will be happier if I do that', not through words, through imagination, through formulas—but if you see the truth of it, you are there. Then there is no conflict. It happens naturally, like the fruit on a tree that ripens.

Questioner: What is the relationship between the body and thought?

Krishnamurti: If I had no body, would I be able to think? Without the body, all the organism with its nerves, its sensitivity, all the operative mechanical processes of the physical system, without that would there be thinking? If I had no brain, the cells that hold memory, which is connected with the whole body through the nerves, would there be thinking?

When the body dies, what happens to the thought we have created? I have lived thirty, fifty, or a hundred years, spending most of my time working in an office—God knows why—earning a livelihood, fighting, quarrelling, bickering, jealous, anxious. You know, my life, the dreadful thing that I live. All that is me. Is that 'me' different from the body? Go into it very carefully. Is that 'me' different from the instrument? Obviously, it is different. The 'me' is the result of my remembering the hurts, the pain, the pleasure, all that, the remembrance, which is stored up in the cells as thought. Will that thought go on when the body dies? You ask the question: When my brother or my friend whom I have remembered, loved, with whom I have walked and enjoyed things, dies—do I remember him and does he exist? I am attached to him and I don't want to lose him. I have lost him physically, but I don't want to lose him. See what takes place. I don't want to lose him, I have a great memory of experience, pleasure, pain, about him or her, I am attached to that, and I hold onto that.

So thought says, 'He does live, we will meet next life, or we will meet in heaven. I like that idea, it gives me comfort'—and you come along and say, 'What nonsense, you are just a superstitious old man', and I fight you because this gives me great comfort. So what I am seeking is comfort, not the truth of anything, but comfort. Now, if I do not seek comfort in any form—what is the fact? If I have lived a shoddy, petty, jealous, anxious life, as millions of people do, what is the importance of me? I am like the vast ocean of people. I die. But I cling to my little life, I want it to continue, hoping that at some future date, I will be happy. And with that idea I die. And I am like a million others in a vast ocean of existence, without meaning, without significance, without beauty, without anything real. And if the mind steps out of that vast stream, as it must, then there is a totally different dimension. And that is the whole process of living: to move away from this vast current of ugliness and brutality. And because we can't do it, we haven't got the energy, the vitality, the intensity, the love of it, we move along with the stream.

Brockwood Park, 9 September 1972

ONE CAN SEE for oneself, if one has observed, how thought, however subtle, has bred this extraordinary human structure of relationship, social behaviour, division; and where there is division, there must be conflict, violence. Whether it is a linguistic or class difference, or the difference brought about by ideologies or systems, such divisions invariably must create violence. And until one learns very deeply how this violence has come about, not merely the cause of violence but going far beyond that, much farther beyond the causation, we shall never, at least it seems to me, be free of this extraordinary misery, confusion, and violence that is going on in the world.

So I am asking myself and we will ask each other: What is freedom in relation to thought and human behaviour? Because it is our behaviour in daily life that is bringing about this chaos in the world. So can there be complete freedom, freedom from thought? And if there is freedom from thought, then what place has thought? Please, this is not intellectual philosophy. Philosophy means the love of truth, not speculative opinion, theoretical conclusion or theoretical perception. Its real meaning is the love of truth in our daily life and behaviour. And to go into this very seriously—and I hope you will do that—one has to inquire, learn, and not memorize something which we think is true or about which we have come to a conclusion—because we are not going to come to any conclusion.

On the contrary, truth isn't a conclusion. A conclusion takes place only when thought produces opinions, dialectical truths. With its conclusion thought then becomes a means of separation.

So what we ought to do is to find out for ourselves and therefore learn what thinking is, and whether thinking, however rational, however logical, sane, objective, can bring about a psychological revolution in our behaviour. Thought is always conditioned, because thought is the response of memory, experience, knowledge, accumulation. Thought springs from that conditioning, and therefore thought can never bring about right behaviour. Do we see this? Because I have met many psychologists throughout the world who, seeing what human beings are actually, how contradictory their behaviour is, what unhappy miserable beings they are, are saying that what we ought to do is to reward them and thereby condition them in a different way. That is, instead of punishing them for their bad behaviour, reward them for good behaviour and forget their bad behaviour. So from childhood you are conditioned by reward in this way to behave rightly, or what they think is rightly—not antisocially. They are still living with thought. To them thought is tremendously important, and like the Communists and others, they say thought must be shaped, thought must be conditioned, in a different way, and from that different structure there will be different behaviour. But they are still living within the pattern of thinking.

This has been tried in ancient India, by the Buddhists; every religion has tried this. But human behaviour, with all its contradictions, its fragmentation, is the result of thought. And if we would change that human behaviour radically—not at the periphery, at the outer edges of our human existence, but at the very core of our being—then we must go into the question of thought. *You* must see this, not I. You must see the truth of this: that thought must be understood, one must learn all about it. It must be tremendously important to you, not because the speaker says so. The speaker has no value whatsoever. What has value is what you are learning, and not memorizing. If you merely repeat what the speaker says, either accepting or denying, then you haven't really gone into the problem at all. Whereas if you really want to solve this human problem of how to live in peace with love, without fear, without violence, you must go into this.

So how is one to learn what freedom is? Not freedom from oppression, freedom from fear, freedom from all the little things that we worry about, but freedom from the very cause of fear, from the very cause of our antagonism, from the very root of our being, in which there is this appalling contradiction, this frightening pursuit of pleasure, and all the gods we have created, with all their churches and priests—you know all the rest of the business. So one has to ask oneself, it seems to me, whether you want freedom at the periphery or at the very core of your being. And if you want to learn what freedom is at the very source of all existence, then you have to learn about thought. If that question is clear—not the verbal explanation, not the idea that you gather from the explanation—but if that is what you feel is the real absolute necessity, then we can travel together. Because if we could understand this, then all our questions will be answered.

So one has to find out what learning is. First, I want to learn whether there is freedom from thought—not how to use thought, that is the next question. But can the mind ever be free from thought? What does this freedom mean? We only know freedom from something—freedom from fear, from this or that, from anxiety, from a dozen things. And is there a freedom which is not *from* anything, but freedom per se, in itself? And in asking that question, is the reply dependent on thought? Or is freedom the non-existence of thought? And learning means instant perception, therefore learning does not require time. I don't know if you see this. Please, this is really fascinatingly important!

Saanen, 15 July 1973

I HOPE YOU and I see the same thing, understand not only verbally but also non-verbally that for these problems, whatever they be—economic, social, religious, personal—we need a mind and heart that is not put together by thought. Thought is not going to solve our problems, because these problems have come into being through the activities of thought. And to bring about a fundamental, radical, revolutionary, psychological change is our main problem.

From *Krishnamurti on Education*

To END THOUGHT I have first to go into the mechanism of thinking. I have to understand thought completely, deep down in me. I have to examine every thought, without letting one thought escape without being fully understood, so that the brain, the mind, the whole being, becomes very attentive. The moment I pursue every thought to the root, to the end completely, I will see that thought ends by itself. I do not have to do anything about it because thought is memory. Memory is the mark of experience; and as long as experience is not fully, completely, totally understood, it leaves a mark. The moment I have experienced completely, the experience leaves no mark. So if we go into every thought and see where the mark is and remain with that mark as a fact—then that fact will open and that fact will end that particular process of thinking, so that every thought, every feeling, is understood. So the brain and the mind are being freed from a mass of memories. That requires tremendous attention, not attention only to the trees and birds, but inward attention to see that every thought is understood.

Saanen, 28 July 1974

CAN THE MIND empty itself of the past and come upon that area of itself which is not touched by thought? You see, we have only operated, so far, within the areas of thought, as knowledge. Is there any other part, any other area of the mind, which includes the brain, which is not touched by human struggle, pain, anxiety, fear, and all the violence, all the things that man has made through thought? The discovery of that area is meditation. That implies the discovery as to whether thought can come to an end, but yet for thought to operate when necessary in the field of knowledge? We need knowledge, otherwise we cannot function, we would not be able to speak, nor be able to write, and so on. Knowledge is necessary to function, and its functioning becomes neurotic when status becomes all important, which is the entering of thought as the 'me', as status. So knowledge is necessary and yet meditation is to discover, or come upon, or to observe, an area in which there is no movement of thought. Can the two live together, harmoniously, daily? That is the problem; not breathing, not sitting straight, not repeating mantras, paying a hundred dollars to learn some ugly little word, and repeating that until you think you are in heaven—which is transcendental nonsense!

Saanen, 24 July 1975

Now, WHAT IS the reason for building the structure called the 'me'? Why has thought done this? This is really an extraordinarily important question, because it is our life. We have to take this desperately seriously. Why has thought created the 'me'? If you see the fact that thought has built the 'me', or if you say the 'me' is something divine, something that existed before all time—which many do say—we have to investigate this too.

Why has thought created the 'me'? Why? I don't know, I am going to find out. Why do you think thought has created the 'me'?

There are two things. One is, thought demands stability, because only where there is security can this be satisfying to the brain. That is, where there is security, the brain operates marvellously, either neurotically or reasonably. So one of the reasons is that thought, being insecure in itself, fragmented in itself, broken up in itself, has created the 'me' as something permanent, the 'me' which has become separate from thought, and therefore thought recognizes it as something permanent. And this permanency is identified through attachment: my house, my character, my wish, my desire, all that gives a complete sense of security and continuity to the 'me'. Isn't that so? And the idea that the 'me' is something before thought—is that so? And who can ever say that it existed before thought? If you say it existed before thought—as many do—then on what reasoning, on what basis, do you assert that? Is it an assertion of tradition, of belief, of not wanting to recognize that the 'me' is a product of thought, but something marvellously divine—which again is a projection of thought that the 'me' is permanent?

So having observed, one puts away the idea that the 'me' is everlastingly divine, everlastingly timeless, or whatever it is, that is too absurd. One can see very clearly that thought has built the 'me'—the 'me' that has become independent, the 'me' that has acquired knowledge, the 'me' that is the observer, the 'me' which is the past. The 'me' which is the past passes through the present and modifies itself as the future; it is still the 'me' put together by thought, and that 'me' has become independent of thought. Right? Shall we go on from there? Please, don't accept the description, the words, but see the *truth* of this thing. As you see the fact of the microphone, see that thing. That 'me' has a name, a form. The 'me' has a label, called *K* or *John*, and it has its form, it identifies with the body, the face, the whole business. So there is the identification of the 'me' with the name and the form, which is the structure, and with the ideal which it wants to pursue, or the desire to change the 'me' into another form of 'me', with another name. So this is the 'me'. That 'me' is the product of time and therefore thought. That 'me' is the word. Remove the word, what is the 'me'?

So that 'me' suffers. The 'me', as the 'you', suffers. So the 'me', in suffering, is 'you'. The 'me' in its great anxiety is the great anxiety of the 'you'—therefore you and I are common. That is the basic essence. Though you are taller, shorter, more clever, have a different temperament, different character—all that is the peripheral movement of culture, but deep down, basically, we are the same.

So that 'me' is moving in the stream of greed, in the stream of selfishness, in the stream of fear, anxiety, and so on, which is the same as you in the stream. That is: you are selfish and another is selfish, you are frightened and another is frightened—basically— you are aching, suffering, tears, greed, envy—that is the common lot of all human beings. That is the stream in which we are living in the present. That is the stream in which we are caught—all of us. Let's put it this way—in that stream we are living, the stream of selfishness. That word includes all the descriptions of the 'me' just given. And when we die the organism dies but the selfish stream goes on.

Consider it. Suppose I have lived a very selfish life, in self-centred activity: my desires, the importance of my desires, the ambitions, the greed, the envy, the accumulation of property, the accumulation of knowledge, the accumulation of all kinds of things that I have gathered—which I have termed as selfishness. And that is the thing I live in, that is the 'me' and that is you also. In our relationship it is the same. So, while living, we are together flowing in the stream of selfishness. This is a fact, not my opinion, not my conclusion. If you observe it, you will see it. When you go to America, you see the same phenomena, in India, all over Europe, modified by the environmental pressures and so on—but basically that is the movement. And when the body dies, the movement goes on.

So this vast stream of selfishness, if I may use that word to include all the things it implies, is the movement of time; and when the body dies, that goes on. We live in that stream in our daily life until we die, and when we die that stream continues. That stream is time. That is the movement of thought that has created suffering, that has created the 'me', from which the 'me' has now asserted itself as being independent and dividing itself from you, but that 'me' is the same as you when it suffers. So the 'me' is the word, the 'me' is the imagined structure of thought. In itself it has no reality. It is what thought has made it; because thought needs security, certainty, it has invested in the 'me' all its certainty. And in that there is suffering. While we are living, we are being carried in that movement, that stream of selfishness. When we die that stream continues to exist.

Is it possible for that stream to end? I die physically, that is obvious. My wife may cry about it, but the fact is I die, the body dies. And this movement of time is going on, of which we are all part. That is why the world is me and I am the world. And will there be an end to this stream, and is it the manifestation of something totally different from the stream? That means, can selfishness, with all its subtleties, come totally to an end? And the ending is the ending of time, and therefore there is a totally different manifestation—which is no selfishness at all.

Saanen, 13 July 1976

WE WERE TALKING about the movement of thought, how thought has built this modern world, both technologically and psychologically, what it has done in the field of science and in the field of psychology. And it has built various religions, various sects, beliefs, dogmas, rituals, saviours, gurus, and all the rest of that business with which you are quite familiar. And we said, thought has its place, limited, fragmented, but thought cannot possibly comprehend or understand or come upon that which is whole. Thought can never find out that which is timeless, if there is a reality, if there is truth. Thought can never, in any circumstances, come upon that immensity; and without the comprehension of that totality, of that dimension in which time as thought and measure does not exist, thought must find its own place and limit itself to that space.

❖

I WOULD LIKE now, if I may, to go into the problem of observing ourselves. When we observe ourselves we are not isolating ourselves, limiting ourselves, becoming self-centred, because, as we explained, we are the world and the world is us. This is a fact. And when we, as human beings, examine the whole content of our consciousness, of ourselves, we are really inquiring into the whole human being—whether he lives in Asia, Europe, or America. So it is not a self-centred activity. When we are observing ourselves, we are not becoming selfish, self-centred, becoming more and more neurotic, lopsided; on the contrary, we are examining, when we look at ourselves, the whole human problem of misery, conflict, and the appalling things that man has made for himself and for others. So it is very important to understand this fact, that we are the world and the world is us. You may have superficial mannerisms, superficial tendencies, but basically all human beings throughout this unfortunate world go through misery, confusion, turmoil, violence, despair, agony. So there is a common ground upon which we all meet. So when we observe ourselves, we are observing human beings.

Madras, 31 December 1977

W HY HAS THOUGHT become so tremendously important? If thought creates fear, if thought has made the past, which is knowledge, so tremendously important, is it possible to give thought its right place so that it does not enter into any other field? Are we communicating?

So what is thinking? When I ask you that question, are you thinking or are you *listening?* Which is it that you are doing? Giving thought its right place gives you freedom from fear. Are you actually listening to that statement? Or are you saying, 'How am I to put thought in its right place, please tell me what to do'? So you are not actually listening! You have turned off, right?

Please listen, find out, learn the art of putting everything in life in its right place—sex, emotion, everything. We are asking: Can thought realize itself and its activities and so bring about its right place? You understand? Thought is now moving in all directions, and one of the directions is fear. So to understand fear, you must understand the place of thought—not stop thought. You may try to, but you can't stop thought. But if you can put it in its right place—not you, when thought puts itself in its right place—then it has understood, it knows its limitation, it knows its capacity to reason, logic, and so on, but in its right place. So we are asking: Can you—can thought—see itself, its own limitation, its own capacity, and say, 'This reason, capacity, has its place and it has no place anywhere else'? Because love is not thought, is it? Is love the product of thought, remembrance?

Remembrance of your sexual or other pleasures—is that love? We are saying that you have to learn, not memorize, not repeat what the speaker has said, but actually find out for yourself whether thought has its own, realizes its own place, and when it realizes it, it won't move in any other direction, and therefore there is no fear. This requires application—testing, not verbal agreement, but daily testing, so that you understand that—not 'you'—thought has created the 'you'. Right? Thought has made you different from itself, and that is one of our problems. The origin of thought is the beginning of remembrance. Whether it is primitive man or the anthropoid ape, remembrance is the beginning of thinking. As a tape registers, the brain registers, which means it remembers. And the origin of thinking is remembering. That is a simple, ordinary fact. So can thought awaken to itself, know itself as the cause of fear, and say: I know my right place. You know, this requires great—not concentration—great awareness of the implications of the whole movement of fear, the understanding of the movement of thought.

You see, if you do this, if your thought goes into it, this is part of real meditation, because you cannot meditate if your life is not in order. If your daily life is not in perfect order, then meditation is something cheap, an escape, a meaningless, illusory pursuit. That is why we are saying if there is to be real meditation, in the full meaning of that word, the depth of that state, the beauty and the clarity and the compassion, you must begin by laying the foundation of order in your daily life. But you find that extremely difficult. Therefore you go off and sit under a tree or hold your nose and do all kinds of stuff thinking you are meditating.

So there is a tremendous possibility of being completely free of fear if you have listened very carefully to what the speaker has said, because we are journeying, walking together, we are sharing together in our walk, in our exploration. Therefore there is no learning from somebody. You are learning as you walk, as you explore. There is no authority. So, now, has thought realized its place?

Meditate upon it. Think about it. Go into it. Give half an hour of your life to find out—not half an hour, give your *life* to find out! Because then you will see for yourself, as a human being who represents mankind, whose consciousness is the consciousness of humanity, when there is no fear in that consciousness you, who have understood and gone beyond it, change the consciousness of humanity. This is a fact. So if I may ask, have you—has thought—learned the art of putting itself in its right place? Then, once it has done that, the doors of heaven are open.

Madras, 7 January 1978

WE ARE TRYING to find out the inmost nature of the self because all our activity is based on self, the 'me' first and you second. In all our relationships, in all our office activities, social activities, in our relationship with each other, self-centred activity is constantly in operation, even when we are meditating, even when we are supposed to be religious. So what is the self? Unfortunately, most of you probably have read philosophy, sacred books—I won't call them sacred because they are just books—or somebody has told you, your guru or your religious leader has probably told you the self is something extraordinary, it is to live everlastingly from the beginning to the end.

So we are asking a very simple question, which is really tremendously complex. How you approach that question matters a great deal: whether you approach it with fear, with a conclusion, or accepting the authority of others, and your approach then is already limited, circumscribed; or whether you see that to investigate one must be free, otherwise you can't investigate. If you are prejudiced, if you have some ideal, conclusion, wish, then that is going to dictate your investigation. So can you, if I may ask, be free to go into this matter very carefully, logically, sanely, and freely, to find out the nature and the inmost essence of the self? ... Though his form, name, may be different, is the individual, the identity of a human being who feels, or thinks he is separate, actually separate? His idiosyncrasies, character, eccentricities, tendencies, qualities—are they the result of the culture in which he is born, or the development of character as a resistance to the culture? This is very, very important.

So first, what are you? Your activity is based on the self, on self-centred activity from morning until night. So what is that centre from which you are acting, the centre from which you are meditating, if you meditate—I hope you don't—the centre from which all your fears, all your anxieties, sorrows, griefs, pain, and affections arise, the centre from which you are seeking happiness, enlightenment, God, or truth, or whatever, the centre from which you say, 'I take a vow to be a monk', the centre from which, if you are in business, you are trying to become more powerful, richer? That is the centre which we are examining, the self. What is that self and how has it come into being? Is it possible to know yourself as you actually are, not what you *think* you are, what you hope to be? Is it possible to know it completely, the essence of it, and is it possible to go beyond all the fragmented activity of the self?

So is the self, that centre, put together by thought? Please think and investigate, reason as though you are thinking about it for the first time; then it is fresh, then you can investigate. But if you say, 'I already know what the self is, I have already come to certain conclusions about it', you will prevent yourself from examining it.

So what is the self? What are you? Not who are you, but actually what are you? There is a difference between who you are and what you are. When you say *who* you are, you are investigating somebody leading further and further away from the centre; but if you say *what* you actually are, 'what is', then you are dealing with actuality. The actuality is that which is actually happening. So what are you? You are a name, a form, the result of a society, a culture which has emphasized throughout the ages that you are separate, something indefinitely identifiable. Right? You have your character, your particular tendency, either aggressive or yielding. Is that not put together by the culture which has been brought about by thought? It is very difficult for people to accept a very simple, logical examination, because they would like to think that the self is something most extraordinary. We are pointing out that *the self is nothing but words and memories.* So *the self is the past.* And to know oneself means to observe oneself, actually what you are, in your relationship with another. Then the reactions of the self come out in our relationship, whether intimate or not intimate. Then you begin to see what you are, your reactions, prejudices, conclusions, ideals, your this and that. Is not all that a result? That which is a result has a cause. So is the cause a series of memories, remembrances, and so a centre that has been created by thought *to which thought clings?*

❖

SO WHAT THEN is love? And what is the real meaning of meditation? Is it the emptying of this consciousness with all its content— fear, greed, envy, nationality, my God and your God, my rituals and my possessions, emptying the whole of that? That means facing, observing nothing. That nothing is not-a-thing. You know, nothing means not-a-thing. A thing is that which has been put together by thought. I wonder if you see all this. Nature has not been put together by thought; the tree, the stars, the waters, and the lovely evening and the beauty of sunlight, have not been put there by thought. But thought has made out of the tree a chair, a table, that is a thing. So when we say nothing, it means not a thing put there by thought. It is not negation.

So what is love? Is it a thing of thought, a fragmentary affair; or when thought is not, then love is? And what relationship has love to sorrow and sorrow to passion? And what is the meaning of death? Love is not a thing, something put together by thought. If thought were love, then that love would be fragmentary, something that thought as desire made acceptable, as pleasure, whether sensory, sexual, or other forms of pleasure. So if love is not thought, then what is the relationship of love to compassion? Does compassion come into being with the ending of sorrow? And what does sorrow mean? Please, you have to understand, this is our life, our daily life that we are talking about. Because we all go through great sorrow—sorrow at the death of someone, different forms and multiple forms of sorrow, agony, loneliness, utter despair, without any hope. How do you think all those poor people without any hope . . . ?

So one has to explore this question of sorrow, whether it is possible to end it completely. This has been one of the things mankind throughout the ages has tried to understand, accept, go beyond, rationalize, or explain by using various Sanskrit words, or putting all sorrow, as the Christians do, onto one person. If you don't do any of that, which are all escapes, you are faced with your sorrow. You know the sorrow of loneliness, don't you, the sorrow of frustration, loving somebody when it is not reciprocated, or the sorrow that comes when you love somebody and he has gone, the sorrow that everyone has, feeling totally, inwardly empty, worthless, without self-sufficiency? You know the various forms of sorrow. Is sorrow self-pity? I have lost somebody, and that brings great agony. In that agony there is self-pity, loneliness, lack of companionship, the sense of being left completely without any strength, vitality, independence. You are totally lonely. We all know this kind of sorrow. By rationalizing, explaining, seeking to escape, which we do, we are caught in a network of escapes. If you don't escape because you understand the futility of escapes, suppression, going off to temples, and all that nonsense, then you are faced with the fact, and do not move from that fact. You understand, 'Do not move'. Thought wants to run away from it, but remain with it, to observe the thing growing, flowering and decaying. And it can only do that when you watch it, when you care for that thing which you call sorrow.

You know when you care for something, you watch it with great tenderness, great care, great attention. A mother looks after her baby, gets up at midnight, many times, weary, but she cares, she is watching! So if, in the same way, you watch this thing called sorrow with care, hesitancy, affection, then you will see there is no escape from it, and that very thing that has been called sorrow turns into some totally different thing, which is passion. Not lust, but passion. And without passion life has no meaning.

So the self and the structure of the self are based on nothing. The innermost depth of the self is absolutely not-a-thing. And the beauty, the greatness, the magnitude of love is only possible when thought realizes it has no place in relationship—and therefore love is.

So the next thing is to find out what is the relationship of love to death. What is the relationship of our existence to death? We are tremendously concerned with what happens after death, but never concerned with what happens before. We are never concerned with how we live our life, but are always concerned with how we end life. Now, we are going to reverse the process and see how you live your daily life, whether in that daily life there is an ending, an ending to your attachment. You know what your life is, don't you? It is one battle from the moment you are born until you die, a series of endless conflicts, of hopeless endeavours leading nowhere but more money, more pleasure, more things—things including your gods because they are made by hand or the mind, which is the activity of thought, anxiety, depression, elation, confusion, uncertainty, always seeking security and never finding it. This is your daily life, controlling yourself, controlling or indulging in sex, ambition, greed, power, position. Right? This is your daily, ugly, brutal life. And you gloss it over by calling it various names and giving peculiar meaning to it. But in actuality this is your daily life and you are afraid to let that go. You are bound to let it go when you die, you can't argue with death. Death through accident, disease, old age, senility, you know, you will face all that.

So this is your life, and we are saying this is far more important than death—not at the end, but now. Death means—please listen—ending. I know you would like to go on. We think there is reincarnation, maybe. Whether there is life hereafter or not is totally irrelevant. What is totally relevant is what is now, whether you can alter the way you live now. Even if you do believe in this idea of reincarnation, *what* is being born next life, *who* is being born? Your self, your greed, your envy, your brutality, your violence modified? And if you believe in that, then what you do now matters enormously, but you don't really go as far as that, you play with the idea, you are greedy, envious, brutal, competitive.

So we are asking whether death means that the brain, without oxygen, without blood, decays, ends. Now, can you end in life now something which you hold most dear, which is your self? Can you end your attachment? End it, not argue about it, end it and see what happens. If you end all the things like greed, envy, anxiety, loneliness, *now,* death has a totally different meaning. Then there is no death, you are living with death all the time. Death is life, ending is a beginning. If you keep the same thing going on continuously, there is nothing new. Only when there is an ending does a flowering take place. You understand? Do it, please, in your life, do it. Test it out. That's what I mean when I say that you must be serious. It is only the serious man who lives; serious in the sense he knows he is frightened, greedy, he is aware of his own peculiar pleasure, and without argument, without suppression, he ends it— with ease, with grace, with beauty. Then you will see a totally different beginning. Because then there is an actual facing of nothing, which is death, which is to invite death while living. That invitation is the ending of all your attachments.

Then out of all this comes a strange factor, the factor of supreme intelligence. That intelligence is based on compassion and clarity, and because of that intelligence there is great skill. So if you are serious, then act, do, not pursuing some vague theory or ideal, but end something that you hold most dear—your ambition, whether your spiritual, physical, or business ambition—end it. Then you will see for yourself a new flowering takes place.

Ojai, 15 May 1980

Questioner: What is the relationship of attention to thought? Is there a gap between attention and thought?

Krishnamurti: This is a good question because it affects us. That is: What is attention, what is the relationship of thought to attention, is there freedom in attention? We know what concentration is, most of us from childhood are trained to concentrate, and what that concentration implies is narrowing down all our energy to a particular point, and holding to that point. A boy at school is looking out the window at a squirrel climbing a tree, and the educator says, 'Look, you are not paying attention, concentrate on the book. Listen to what I am saying', which is to make concentration far more important than attention. If I were the educator, I would help the boy to watch the squirrel completely, to watch the movement of the tail, how its claws are, everything. Then if he learns to watch that attentively, he will pay attention to the book! So there is no contradiction.

Attention is a state of mind in which there is no contradiction. There is no entity or centre or point which says, 'I must attend'. It is a state in which there is no wastage of energy, whereas in concentration there is always the controlling process going on: I want to concentrate on a page but thought wanders off, and then I pull it back, with a constant battle. Whereas in attention it is very simple really, when somebody says, 'I love you', and he means it, you are attending. You don't say, 'Do you love me because I look nice, or I have money, or for sexual reasons?', or this or that. So attention is something totally different from concentration.

And the questioner asks what the relationship of attention is to thought. None, obviously. Concentration has a relationship to thought because thought directs: 'I must learn, I must concentrate in order to control myself'. Thought gives a direction from one point to another point, whereas in attention thought has no place—I just attend.

And is there a gap between attention and thought? Once you have a grasp of the whole movement of thought, you won't put this question. Understanding what thought is, is not somebody telling you what thought is, but seeing what thought is, how it comes into being?

There can be no thought if there is total amnesia. But we are not in a state of amnesia, and one wants to find out what thought is, what place it has in life. Thinking takes place as a reaction to memory. Memory responds to a challenge, to a question, an action, or in relation to something, an idea, a person. You see all this in life. So one then asks: What is memory? When you have trodden on some insect and it bites you and that pain is registered and stored in the brain, that is memory. That pain which becomes a memory is not actual pain. The pain is over but the memory remains, so the next time you are careful. There is experience as pain, which has become knowledge, and that knowledge, experience, is stored as memory, and that memory responds as thought. Memory is thought. And knowledge, however wide, however deep, however extensive, must always be limited. There is no complete knowledge.

So thought is always partial, limited, divisive, because in itself it isn't complete, it can never be complete; it can *think* about completeness, it can think about totality, the whole, but thought itself is not whole. So whatever it creates philosophically, religiously, is still partial, limited, fragmentary, because knowledge is part of ignorance. As knowledge can never be complete, it must always go hand in hand with ignorance. And if one understands the nature of thought, and what concentration is, then thought cannot attend because attention is giving all your energy without any restraint. If you are attending now, what takes place? There is no 'you' attending. There is no centre that says, 'I must attend'. You are attending because it is your life, your interest. If you are not interested, that's a different matter. But if you are serious and giving attention, you will find that all your problems have gone—at least for the moment.

So to resolve problems is to attend. It's not a trick!

MORE THAN TWO hundred and fifty questions have been sent in, always somehow not dealing with the facts of oneself. You don't ask: Why is my mind chattering, so restless? Have you ever asked that question of yourself, why you are so restless, moving from one thing to another, seeking constant entertainment? Why is your mind chattering? And what will you do about it? Your immediate response is to control it, to say, 'I must not chatter'. Which means what? The very controller is chattering. There is a controller who says, 'I mustn't chatter'; he is himself part of chattering. See the beauty of it! So what will you do?

I don't know if you have noticed that the mind, the whole structure of the brain, must be occupied with something—with sex, with problems, with television, with going to football, going to church. Why must it be occupied? If it is not occupied, aren't you rather uncertain, afraid of not being occupied? You feel empty, don't you? You feel lost, you begin to realize what you are, that there is tremendous loneliness inside. And so to avoid that deep loneliness, with all its agony, the mind chatters, is occupied with everything else except that. And then that becomes the occupation. If I am not occupied with all the outward things, like cooking, washing up, cleaning the house, and so on, it says, 'I am lonely, how am I to get over it, let me talk about it, how miserable I am'—back to chattering. But why is the mind chattering? Ask the question. Why is your mind chattering, with never a moment when it is quiet, never a moment when there is complete freedom from any problem?

Is that occupation the result of our education, the social nature of our life? Those are all excuses, obviously. But realize that your mind is chattering and look at it, work with it, stay with it. If my mind is chattering, I'll watch it. I say, 'All right, chatter', but I am attending to it, which means I am not trying not to chatter. I am not saying I must not suppress it, I am just attending to chattering. If you do, you will see what happens. Then your mind is so clear, free of all this. And probably that is the state of a normal healthy human being.

Discussion with Professor David Bohm at Brockwood Park 14 September 1980

Krishnamurti: Now then, the question is, Is there something beyond all this chaos, which is never touched by human thought, mind?

David Bohm: Yes, that is a difficult point, not touched by the human mind, but mind might go beyond thought.

K: That's what I want to find out.

DB: Then what do you mean—do you mean by the mind only thought, feeling, desire, will, or something much more?

K: No, for the time being we have said that the mind, the human mind, is that.

DB: The mind is now considered to be limited.

K: As long as the human mind is *caught* in that, it is limited.

DB: Yes, but the human mind has potential.

K: Tremendous potential.

DB: Which it does not realize now, it is caught in thought, feeling, desire, will, and that sort of thing.

K: That's right.

DB: Then we'll say that that which is beyond this is not touched by this limited sort of mind. Now, what will we mean by the mind which is beyond this limit?

K: First of all, sir, is there such a mind?

DB: Yes, that's the first question.

K: Is there such a mind that has actually, not theoretically or romantically, all the rest of that nonsense, actually said, 'I've been through this'?

DB: You mean, through the limited stuff.

K: Yes. And being through it means finished with it. Is there such a mind? Or because it *thinks* it has finished with it, therefore creates the illusion that there is something else. I won't accept that. As a human being, one person, or 'X' says, 'I have understood this, I have seen the limitation of all this, I have lived through it, and I have come to the end of it'. And this mind, having come to the end of it, is no longer the limited mind. And is there a mind which is totally limitless?

DB: Yes, now that raises the question of how the brain is able to be in contact with that mind. What is the relation between that unlimited mind and the brain?

K: I'm coming to that. First of all, I want to be clear on this point—

it's rather interesting, if we go into it. This mind, the whole of it, the whole nature and structure of the mind, including the emotions, the brain, the reactions, and the physical responses, has lived in turmoil, in chaos, in loneliness, and has understood, has had a profound insight into all that. And having such a deep insight has cleared the field. *This* mind is no longer *that* mind.

DB: Yes, it's no longer the original limited mind that you began with.

K: Yes, no longer the limited mind, damaged mind. Let's use the word *damaged*.

DB: That you began with.

K: Damaged mind. Let's use the word damaged.

DB: Damaged mind, also damaged brain—its working has damaged the brain.

K: Yes, all right. Damaged mind means damaged emotions, damaged brain.

DB: The cells themselves are not in the right order.

K: Quite. But when there is this insight and therefore order, the damage is undone. I don't know if you agree to that.

DB: Yes, certainly you can see by reasoning that it's quite possible, because you can say the damage was done by disorderly thoughts and feelings which over-excite the cells and disrupt them. And now, with the insight, that stops and a new process is set up.

K: Yes, it's like a person going for fifty years in a certain direction who suddenly realizes that that's not the direction, the whole brain changes.

DB: It changes at the core and then the wrong structure is disman-
tled and healed. That may take time, you said.

K: That's right.

DB: But the insight which . . .

K: . . . is the factor that will change it.

DB: Yes, and that insight does not take time, but it means that the
whole process has changed its origin.

K: That's right. That mind, the limited mind with all its consciousness and its content says that part is over. Now, if it is an actuality
that that mind which has been limited, and having had insight into
this limitation has therefore moved away from that limitation, is it
something that is really tremendously revolutionary? You follow?
And therefore it is no longer the human mind. Forgive me for using
that word.

DB: Well, I think we should clear that up, what we mean by the
human mind.

K: Human mind with its limited consciousness.

DB: Yes, that limited consciousness which is conditioned and not
free.

K: That is ended.

DB: Yes, so that is the general consciousness which has been the
case, I mean, not just in individuals, but it has been all around.

K: Yes, of course, I'm not talking of an individual, that's too silly.

DB: Yes, but I think we discussed that, that the individual is the outcome of the general consciousness, a particular outcome rather than an independent thing. You see, that's one of the difficulties.

K: Yes, that's one of the confusions.

DB: The confusion is that we take the individual mind to be the concrete actuality. We've discussed in the past the need to consider this general mind to be the actuality from which the individual mind is formed.

K: Yes, that's all very clear.

DB: But now you are saying we move away even from that general mind, but what does it mean?

K: Yes, from the general and the particular.

DB: And the particular mind.

K: Now, if one has totally moved away from it, then what is the mind?

DB: Yes, and what is the person, what is the human being? Right?

K: What is a human being then? And then what is the relationship between that mind, which is not man-made, and the man-made mind? I don't know if I'm making myself clear.

DB: Well, did we agree to call it a universal mind, or would you prefer not to?

K: I don't like that word *universal mind*, lots of people have used it. Let's use a much simpler word.

DB: Well, it's the mind not made by man.

K: I think that's simpler, keep it to that, a mind not made by man.

DB: Neither individually nor in general.

K: Generally or individually, it's not made by man. Sir, can one observe, really, deeply, without any prejudice, and all the rest, does such a mind *exist?* You follow what I'm trying to say?

DB: Yes, let's see what it means to observe that. I think there are some difficulties of language here, because you see, we say one must observe, and things like that, whereas . . .

K: I observe it, I observe.

DB: Who observes it, you see, that's one of the problems that comes up.

K: We've been through all that. There is no division in observation. Not I observe, there is only observation.

DB: Observation takes place.

K: Yes.

DB: Would you say it takes place in a particular brain, for example, or a particular brain takes part in the observation?

K: I know the catch in this. No, sir, it doesn't take place in a particular brain.

DB: Yes, but it seems that a particular brain may respond.

K: Of course, but it is not K's brain.

DB: No, I don't mean that. What I mean by the words *particular brain* is that given the particulars of where a certain human being is in space and time or whatever his form is, not giving him a name, we could say he is distinguished from another one which might be there.

K: Look, sir, let's get clear on this point. We live in a man-made world, man-made mind, we are the result of man-made minds, our brains with all their responses and so on.

DB: Well, the brain itself is not man-made but it has been conditioned, by man-made conditioning.

K: Conditioned by man, right, that's what I mean. Now, can that mind uncondition itself so completely that it's no longer man-made? That is the question—let's keep it to that simple level. Can that mind, man-made mind as it is now, can it go to that extent, to so completely liberate itself from itself?

DB: Yes, of course, that's a somewhat paradoxical statement.

K: Of course. Paradoxical, but it's actual, it is so. Let's begin again. One can observe that the consciousness of humanity is its content. And its content is all the man-made things—anxiety, fear, and all the rest of it. And it is not only particular, it is the general. Having had an insight into this, it has cleansed itself from that.

DB: Well, that implies it was always potentially more than that and insight enabled it to be free of that. Is that what you mean?

K: That insight—I won't say it is potential.

DB: Well, there is a little difficulty of language. If you say the brain or the mind had an insight into its own conditioning, then you're almost saying it became something else.

K: Yes, I am saying that, I am saying that. The insight transforms the man-made mind.

DB: Right. So then it's no longer the man-made mind.

K: It's no longer the man-made mind. That insight means the wiping away of all the content of consciousness. Right? Not bit by bit, but the totality of it. And that insight is not the result of man's endeavour.

DB: Yes, but then that seems to raise the question of where does it come from.

K: All right. Where does it come from? Yes, in the brain itself, in the mind itself.

DB: Which, the brain or the mind?

K: Mind, I'm saying the whole if it. Just a minute, sir. Let's go slowly—it's rather interesting, let's go slowly. The consciousness is man-made, general and particular. And logically, reasonably, one sees the limitations of it. Then the mind has gone much further. Then it comes to a point when it says, 'Can all this be wiped away at one breath, one blow, one movement?' And that movement is insight, the movement of insight. It is still in the mind. But not born of that consciousness. I don't know if I'm making myself clear.

DB: Yes. Then you are saying the mind has the possibility, a potential of moving beyond the consciousness.

K: Yes.

DB: But we haven't actually done much of it.

K: Of course. It must be a part of the brain, a part of the mind.

DB: The brain, mind can do that, but it hasn't generally done it.

K: Yes. Now, having done all this, is there a mind which is not man-made, which man cannot conceive, cannot create, and which is not an illusion? Is there such a mind? I don't know if I am making myself clear.

DB: Well, I think what you are saying is, having freed itself the mind has . . .

K: From the general and particular . . .

DB: . . . freed itself from the general and particular structure of consciousness of mankind, from its limits, and this mind is now much greater. Now you say that this mind is raising a question.

K: This mind is raising a question.

DB: Which is what?

K: Which is, first, is that mind free from the man-made mind? That's the first question.

DB: It may be an illusion.

K: Illusion—that's what I want to get at, one has to be very clear. No, it is not an illusion, because he sees measurement is an illusion, he knows the nature of illusions and that where there is desire there must be illusions. And illusions must create limitation, and so on. He's not only understood it, he's over it.

DB: He's free of desire.

K: Free of desire. That is the nature. I don't want to put it so brutally. Free of desire.

DB: But it is full of energy.

K: Yes, so this mind, which is no longer general and particular, and therefore not limited, the limitation having been broken down through insight, is no longer that conditioned mind. Then what is that mind? Being aware that it is no longer caught in illusion.

DB: Yes, but you were saying it was raising a question about whether there is something much greater.

K: Yes, that's why I'm raising the question.

DB: Whatever that may be.

K: Yes. Is there a mind which is not man-made? And if there is, what is its relationship to the man-made mind? This is very difficult. You see every form of assertion, every form of verbal statement is not that. Right? So we're asking, is there a mind which is not man-made. And I think that can only be asked when the other, when the limitations are ended, otherwise it's just a foolish question.

DB: It'll be the same . . .

K: Just a waste of time. I mean, that becomes theoretical, nonsensical.

DB: Part of the man-made structure.

K: Of course, of course. So one must be absolutely, one must be . . .

DB: I think the word *absolute* can be used there if we are very careful.

K: Very careful, yes. Absolutely free of all this. Then only can you put that question. Is there a mind that is not man-made and if there is such a mind, what is its relationship to the man-made mind? Now, is there such a mind, first? Of course there is. Of course, sir. Without being dogmatic or personal or all that business, there is. But it is not God.

DB: Right, well.

K: Because God—we've been through all that.

DB: That is part of the man-made structure.

K: Which has created chaos in the world. So there is. Then, the next question is, if there is such a mind, and someone says there is, what is the relationship of that to the man-made mind?

DB: Yes, the general.

K: The particular and the general. Has it any relationship?

DB: Well, the question is a difficult one because you could say that the man-made mind is pervaded with illusion, most of its content is not real.

K: No, and this is real.

DB: Actual or whatever.

K: We'll use the world *real* in the sense actual, and that is measurable, confused—has *this* any relationship to *that?* Obviously not.

DB: Well, I would say a superficial one in the sense that the man-made mind has some real content at a certain level, a technical level, let's say, the television system and so on.

K: Well . . .

DB: So in that sense there could be a relationship in that area but, as you were saying, that is a very small area. But fundamentally . . .

K: The man-made mind has no relationship to that, but that has a relationship to this.

DB: Yes, but not to the illusions in the man-made mind.

K: Wait a minute, let's be clear. My mind is the man-made mind. It has got illusions, desires and all the rest of it. And there is that other mind which has not, which is beyond all limitations. This illusory mind, the man-made mind, is always seeking that.

DB: Yes, that's its main trouble.

K: That's its main trouble. It is measuring it, it is advancing, getting nearer, farther, all the rest of it. And this mind, the man-made mind, is always seeking that, and therefore it's creating more and more mischief, confusion. This man-made mind has no relationship to that.

DB: Yes, because any attempt to get that is the source of illusion.

K: Of course, of course, obviously. Now, has *that* any relationship to *this?*

DB: Well, what I was suggesting was, that it would have to have, that if we take the illusions which are in that mind such as desire and fear and so on, it has no relationship to that, because they are figments anyway.

K: Yes, understood.

DB: But *that* can have a relationship to the man-made mind in understanding its true structure.

K: Are you saying, sir, that that mind has a relationship to the human mind the moment it's moving away from the limitations?

DB: Yes, but in understanding those limitations, it moves away.

K: Yes, it moves away. Then that has a relationship.

DB: Then it has a genuine relationship to what this limited mind actually is, not to the illusions as to what it thinks it is.

K: Let's be clear.

DB: Well, we have to get the words right—the mind which is not limited, right, which is not man-made, cannot be related to the illusions which are in the man-made mind.

K: No, agreed.

DB: But it has to be related to the source, as it were, to the real nature of the man-made mind, which is behind the illusion.

K: Which is, the man-made mind is based on what?

DB: Well, on all these things we have said.

K: Yes, which is its nature. Therefore how can *that* have a relationship to *this*, even basically?

DB: The only relationship is in understanding it, so that some communication would be possible, which might end, might communicate to the other person . . .

K: No, I'm questioning that.

DB: Because you were saying that the mind that is not man-made may be related to the limited mind, and not the other way round.

K: I even question that.

DB: It may or may not be so, is that what you're saying, by questioning it.

K: Yes, I'm questioning it.

DB: All right.

K: What is the relationship then of love to jealousy? It has none.

DB: Not to jealousy itself, which is an illusion, but to the human being who is jealous, there may be.

K: No, I'm taking love and hatred—two words, love and hatred, love and hatred have no relationship to each other.

DB: No, not really.

K: None, not really.

DB: I think that love might understand the origin of hatred, you see.

K: Ah, it might—yes, yes.

DB: In that sense I would think there is a relationship.

K: I see, I understand. You're saying, love can understand the origin of hatred and how hatred arises and all the rest of it. Does love understand that?

DB: Well, I think in some sense that it understands its origin in the man-made mind, that having seen the man-made mind and all its structure and moved away . . .

K: Are we saying, sir, that love—we will use that word for the moment—that love has a relationship to non-love?

DB: Only in the sense of dissolving it.

K: I'm not sure, I'm not sure, we must be awfully careful here. Or is it the ending of itself... ?

DB: Which is it?

K: The ending of hatred, the other is, not the other has a relationship to the understanding of hatred.

DB: Yes, well, we have to ask how it gets started then, you see.

K: That's very simple.

DB: No, but I mean, supposing we say we have hatred.

K: I have hatred. Suppose I have hatred. I can see the origin of it. Because you insulted me.

DB: Well, that's a superficial notion of the origin, I mean, why does one behave so irrationally is the deeper origin. You see, there's no real—if you merely say you've insulted me, I say why should you respond to the insult?

K: Because all my conditioning is that.

DB: Yes, that's what I mean by your understanding the origin of...

K: I understand that, but does love help me to understand the origin of hatred?

DB: No, but I think that someone in hatred, understanding its origin and moving away . . .

K: . . . then the other is. The other cannot help the movement away.

DB: No, but the question is, suppose one person, if you want to put it that way, has this love and the other has not, can the first one communicate something which will start the movement in the second one?

K: That means A can influence B?

DB: Not influence, but I mean one could raise the question, for example, why should anybody be talking about any of this?

K: That's a different matter—that's a different matter. No, the question, sir, is: Is hate dispelled by love?

DB: No, not that, no.

K: Or with the understanding of hatred and the ending of it, the other is?

DB: That's right, but now, if we say that here in A love now is—right? A has reached that.

K: Yes.

DB: A has love and he sees B . . .

K: B has got the other.

DB: Now, we're saying, what is he going to do, you see, that's the question.

K: What is the relationship between the two?

DB: That's the same question.

K: The same question, yes.

DB: What is he going to do is another way of putting it.

K: I think—just a minute, sir. I hate, another loves. My wife loves and I hate. She can talk to me, she can point it out to me, the unreasonableness and so on, but her love is not going to transform the source of my hatred.

DB: That's clear, yes, except her love is the energy which will be behind the talk.

K: Behind the talk, yes.

DB: The love itself doesn't sort of go in there and dissolve the hate.

K: Of course not—that's romantic and all that business. So the man who hates and has an insight into the source of it, the cause of it, the movement of it, and ends it, has the other.

DB: Yes, I think that we say A is the man who has seen all this and he now has the energy to put it to B—it's up to B what happens.

K: Of course. I think we had better pursue this.

Ojai, 3 May 1981

THE CRISIS IS not in politics, in governments, whether totalitarian or so-called democratic, the crisis is not among the scientists nor among the established respectable religions. The crisis is in our consciousness, which means in our minds, our hearts, our behaviour, our relationship. And the crisis cannot be understood fully, and perhaps met totally, unless we understand the nature and structure of consciousness, which is put together by thought.

SO WE ARE learning, or observing our own state of mind. That's where real education, self-education, begins. We have learned so much from others about ourselves, we are always looking for others to lead us, not only outwardly, but specially in the psychological realm, inwardly. If there is any trouble, any disturbance, we immediately go after somebody who will help us to clear it up. We are addicted to institutions and organizations, hoping that they will settle our problems, help us to clarify our own minds. So we are always depending on somebody; and that dependence will inevitably bring about corruption. So here we are not depending on anybody, including the speaker, particularly not the speaker, because there is no intention to persuade you to think in any particular direction, to stimulate you with fanciful words and theories. Rather, observe what is actually going on in the world, and all the confusion within, and, in so observing, do not make an abstraction of what is observed into an idea. Please, let's be very clear on this point. When we observe a tree, the word *tree* is an abstraction, it is not the tree. I hope that is clear. The word, the explanation, the description, is not the actuality, it is not 'what is'. So we must be very clear on this from the beginning. When we observe what is actually going on in the world and deeply in our own consciousness, that observation can remain pure, direct, clear, when there is no abstraction of what is observed into an idea. Most of us live with ideas, which are not actualities. Ideas then become all important, not what actually is. Philosophers use ideas in various senses, but we are not dealing with ideas. We are concerned only with the observation of what is going on—actually, not theoretically, not according to a particular pattern of thought, but *what is*. And, in that observation of *what is*, to make that very clear. An abstraction of *what is* into an idea brings only further confusion.

As we said, the crisis is in our consciousness, and that consciousness is the common ground of all humanity. It is not a particular consciousness, it is not your consciousness, it is the consciousness of man, of the human being, because wherever you go, the Far East, the Middle East, or the West, all over the world, the human being suffers, has pain, lives in deep uncertainty, loneliness, utter despair, caught in various fanciful religious concepts which have no meaning whatsoever in actuality. So this is common to all mankind. Please do see this very clearly. It is not your consciousness, it is the consciousness of all human beings, who go through such travail, misery, conflict, wanting to identify themselves with something, with the nation, with a religious figure, or a concept.

Please grasp the significance of this. It is very important to understand because we have separated ourselves as individuals, which actually we are not. We are the result of a million years in which we have been encouraged to accept the idea—the *idea*—of the individual. But when you observe closely, you are not an individual, you are like the rest, psychologically, of mankind. This is a very difficult thing to perceive because most of us cling to this idea—*idea*—that we are all separate individuals with our own personal ambitions, greed, envy, suffering, loneliness. But when you observe, this is what everybody is doing. And the concept of an individual makes us much more selfish, self-centred, neurotic, and competitive; competition also is destroying man. So the world is you, and you are the world. That is a marvellous feeling, if you really understand it. There is great vitality, perception, immense beauty in it. Not the mere beauty of a painting, a poem, or a lovely face. But we are the world, and that world is you, me.

And in this part of the world, freedom is misused, just as in the rest of the world, because each one wants to fulfil, to be, to become. And therefore the content of our consciousness is a constant struggle to be, become, succeed, have power, position, status. And you can have that only if you have money, talent, or capacity in a particular direction. So capacity, talent, encourage individuality. But if you observe it, that individuality is put together by thought.

So observing all this, the crisis is in the very nature of thought. The outward world and the inward world are put together by thought. Thought is a material process. Thought has built the atom bomb, the space shuttle, the computer, the robot, and all the instruments of war. Thought has also built the marvellous cathedrals and churches, and everything they contain. But there is nothing whatsoever that is sacred in the movement of thought. What thought has created as a symbol that you worship is not sacred, it is put there by thought. The rituals, all the religious and the national divisions, are the result of thought. Please look at it very closely. We are not persuading, condemning, or encouraging, we are just observing. This is a fact.

So the crisis is in the very nature of thought. And as we have said, thought is the result of the origin of the senses, the sensory responses, the experience, meeting with something which is recorded as knowledge, as memory, and from that memory arises thought. This has been the process and nature of thought for countless years. All culture, from ancient Egypt and before, is based on thought. And thought has created this confusion outside and inside. Please observe it for yourself, I am not teaching you, I am not explaining, the speaker is merely putting this into words in order to communicate what he has observed. We are both observing the nature and the structure of thought. That is, sensory reactions, when you meet with something which is an experience, that experience is recorded as knowledge, that knowledge becomes memory, and that memory acts as thought. So from that action you learn more, accumulate more knowledge. So man has lived for a million years in this process—experience, knowledge, memory, thought, action, in this chain. I wonder if we see this very clearly.

❖

OUR CRISIS THEN is in the very nature of thought. You will say, 'How can we act without knowledge, without thought?' That is not the point. First, observe the nature of thought, very clearly, without any prejudice, without any direction, just see that it is like that. Our brains living in this cycle of experience, knowledge, action, memory, more knowledge, have problems because knowledge is always limited. So our brains are trained to resolve problems. It is a problem-resolving brain, it is never free from problems. One hopes you see the distinction between the two. Our brains have been trained to resolve problems both in the scientific world and in the psychological world, in the world of relationship. Problems arise, we try to solve them. The solution is always sought within the field of knowledge.

As we were saying, knowledge is always incomplete. This is a fact. This is rather an important point to observe, with sensitive awareness, that knowledge is never complete under any circumstances.

Let's look at something else, which is, what is beauty? Because there is so little beauty in the world. Apart from nature, apart from the hills, groves, rivers, birds, and the things of the earth, why is there so little beauty in our lives? We go to the museums and see paintings, sculptures, and the extraordinary things man has made—the poems, the literature, the magnificent architecture, but when we look within there is so little beauty. We want beautiful faces, paint them, but inwardly—we are again observing, not denying or accepting—there is so little sense of beauty, quietness, dignity. Why? Why has man become like this? Why have human beings who are so clever, so erudite in all other directions, going to the moon and planting a piece of cloth up there, creating marvellous machinery, why have all of us become what we are—vulgar, noisy, mediocre, full of vanity over a little career, arrogant in our little knowledge—why? What has happened to mankind? What has happened to you?

And I think this is the crisis. And we avoid it, we don't want to look at ourselves clearly. And self-education is the beginning of wisdom—not in books, not in somebody else, but in the understanding of our own selfish, narrow, distorted activity that is going on day after day, day after day. The crisis is in our heart and mind, in our brain. And as knowledge is always limited, and we are always acting within that field, there is everlasting conflict. This must be clearly understood. We try to solve problems—political, religious, personal relationships, and so on—and these problems are never solved. You try to solve one problem and the very solution of it brings other problems, which is happening in the political world. And so you turn to faith, to belief. I do not know if you have observed that belief atrophies the brain. Look at it, observe it. The constant assertion, 'I believe in God', 'I believe in this', 'I believe in that', the repetition of that, which is what is happening in the churches, the cathedrals, the temples, the mosques, is gradually atrophying the brain, not giving it nourishment. When a person is attached to a belief, a person, or an idea, there is in that attachment conflict, fear, jealousy, anxiety, and that is part of the atrophy of the brain, this constant repetition. I am American, I am British, Hindu, and all that nationalistic nonsense. The repetition of that, if you observe, undernourishes the brain, and so the brain becomes more and more dull, as you must have observed in those people who repeat everlastingly that there is only one saviour, there is only the Buddha, Christ, this or that.

If you watch yourself, you will see this attachment to a belief is part of the desire to be secure, and that the desire and demand for psychological security in any form brings about this atrophying of the brain. From that arise all kinds of neurotic behaviour. Most of us would rather reject this because it is too frightening to observe. That is the very nature of mediocrity. When you go to some guru, priest, or church, and repeat, repeat, repeat, and your meditation is a form of that repetition—in that there is security, a sense of safety, and so gradually your brain becomes atrophied, shrivelled, it becomes small. Watch this for yourself. I am not teaching you. You can observe it in your life. But this observation of the crisis, and the crisis which is in our mind and heart and in our consciousness, is always bringing about conflict because we are never able to solve a single problem completely without having other problems. So look what is happening to us. Problem after problem, crisis after crisis, uncertainty after uncertainty.

So can the brain, mind, ever be free from problems? Please ask this. This is a fundamental question one must ask oneself. But the brain is so trained to solve problems, it cannot understand what it means to be free of problems. Being free it can resolve problems, but not the other way round. . . .

If this is very clear, then one begins to inquire if there is another instrument which will free the brain of all problems so that it can meet problems. You see the difference? It is only the free mind, free brain, that has no problems, that can meet problems and resolve them immediately. But the brain that is trained to the solution of problems, such a brain will always be in conflict. And then the question arises: How is it possible to be free of conflict when, as we have said, thought is the instrument that is creating our problems?

Look at it very closely in another direction. We have problems in relationship between man and woman, or between man and man—homosexuality—in this country and elsewhere. Look at it very closely, observe it, not trying to change it, trying to direct it, saying, it must not be this way, or it must be that way, or help me to get over it, but just observe. You can't change the line of that mountain, or the flight of a bird, or the swift flow of a river, you just observe it, and see the beauty of it. But if you observe and say, that is not as beautiful as the mountain I saw yesterday, you are not observing, you are merely comparing.

So let's observe very closely this question of relationship. Relationship is life. One cannot exist without relationship. You may deny relationship, you may withdraw from relationship because it is frightening, because there is conflict, hurt in it. So most of us build a wall round ourselves in relationship. But let's look very closely, observe, not learn—there is nothing to learn, only observing. Do you see the beauty of it? Because we always want to learn and put it into the category of knowledge. Then we feel safe. Whereas if you observe without any direction, without any motive, without any interference of thought, just observe, not only with a naked eye visually, but also with a mind, heart, and brain that are free to observe without any prejudice, then you discover for yourself the beauty of relationship. But we have not that beauty. So let's look at it closely.

What is relationship? To be related, not blood relationship, but to be related to another. Are we ever related to another? . . . Psychologically, inwardly, deeply, are we ever related to anybody at all? Or we want to be so deeply related and we don't know how it could happen. So our relationship with another is full of tears, occasional joy, occasional pleasure, and the repetition of sexual pleasure.

So, if you observe, are we related to anybody at all? Or are you related to another through thought, through the image that thought has built about your husband or your wife, the image that you have about her or him? So our relationship is between the image you have about her and she has about you. And each one carries this image, and each one goes in his own direction—ambition, greed, envy, competition, seeking power, position. You know what is happening in relationship, each one moving in opposite or perhaps parallel directions, and never meeting. Because this is modern civilization, this is what you are offering to the world. So there is constant struggle, conflict, divorce, changing of so-called mates. You know what is happening.

When you observe all this it is rather frightening, and this is called freedom. But when you observe the fact—if you observe the fact very closely without any motive, without any direction, the fact begins to change because you are giving your complete attention to observing. Do you follow this? When you give complete attention to something, you bring light upon the subject. Then that light clarifies, and that clarification dissolves that which is. Do you understand this? Are we meeting each other? The fact is there is an image which thought has created over five, twenty, or thirty days, or ten years. And the other has an image and each one is ambitious, greedy, wanting to fulfil sexually, this way, that way; you know, all the turmoil that goes on in so-called relationship. And to observe that, pure observation of that. It is only when you want to escape from it that all the neurotic business begins, and then you have all the psychologists helping you to become more neurotic. Face the problem, look at it, give your total attention to it. When you do give such complete attention, with your heart, your brain, your nerves, with everything you have, giving all your energy to look, then in that attentive observation there is clarification. And that which is clear has no problem. Then relationship becomes something entirely different.

So life, for most of us, is becoming an enormous problem, because life is relationship. If we are not related, as we are not, from that all problems arise. We have created a society which is born out of the lack of relationship. And the Communists, the socialists, all the politicians, are trying to change the nature and the structure of society. The basic question is to have right relationship with another. If you have it with one person you have it with everybody, with nature, with all the beauty of the earth.

So one has to inquire very deeply into why thought has created this havoc in our lives, because it is thought that has put together this image of my wife and myself, or of me and another. You cannot escape from this unless you resolve it, look at it—going to church, praying, that is all too childish, utterly immature, because it hasn't solved anything. One must begin very close to go very far. To begin very close is to observe our relationship with another, who-ever it is—with your boss, your carpenter, your foreman, your husband—for life is a movement in relationship. We have destroyed that relationship by thought. And thought is not love. Love is not pleasure, it is not desire. But we have reduced everything to that.

Rajghat, 25 November 1981

WE HAVE TO inquire first not only into what is religion, but what is thought, what is thinking? Because all our activities, our imaginings, all the things written down in the Upanishads, or other religious books, are put together by thought. The architecture, the extraordinary technology in the world, all the temples and the things they contain, whether a Hindu temple, a mosque, a church, are the result of thought. All the rituals, the puja, worship are invented by thought. Nobody can deny that. All our relationship is based on thought, all our political structure is based on thought, the economic structure, our national divisions, are the result of thought. You see, we have always inquired into the external things but we have never asked ourselves: What is thinking? What is the root and what are the consequences of thinking? Not what you think *about*, but the *movement* of thinking, not the *result* of thinking, which is different from inquiry into thinking itself. Are we together in this?

❖

THINKING IS COMMON to all mankind. Thought is not my thought, there is only thought, neither oriental or occidental, East or West, there is only thinking.

Now we will explain what thinking is, but the explanation is not the actual awareness of how thought arises in yourself. The speaker can go into it, describe it, but that explanation is not your own understanding of the origin of thinking. The verbal description is not your actual discovery, but through explanation, through verbal communication, you yourself discover it. That is far more important than the speaker's explanation.

The speaker has talked a great deal throughout the world for the last sixty years. So they have invented a term called 'his teachings' [laughter]. Just a minute. The teachings are not something out there in a book; what the teachings say is, 'Look at yourself, go into yourself, inquire into what is there, understand it, go beyond it', and so on. The teachings are only a means of pointing, explaining, but you have to understand, not the teachings, but *yourself*. Is that clear? So please don't try to understand what the speaker is saying, but understand that what he is saying is acting as a mirror in which you are looking at yourself When you look at yourself very carefully, then the mirror is not important, you throw it away. So that is what we are doing.

What is thinking, upon which you all depend for your livelihood, in your relationships, in your search for something beyond itself? It is very important to understand the nature of thought. The speaker has discussed this matter with many Western scientists, who have gone into the question of the brain. We are only using a very small part of the whole brain. You can observe this in yourself if you have gone into it; that is part of meditation, to find out for yourself whether the whole brain is operating, or only one very small part. That is one of the questions. Thought is the response of memory, memory has been stored through knowledge, knowledge is gathered through experience. That is, experience, knowledge, memory stored in the brain, then thought, then action; from that action you learn more—that is, you accumulate more experience, more knowledge, and so store more memory in the brain, and then act, from that action learn more. So the whole process is based on this movement: experience, knowledge, memory, thought, action.

This is our pattern of living, which is thought. There is no dispute about this. We gather a lot of information through our experience, or through others' experience, store up this knowledge in our brain, from which thought arises, and act. Man has done this for the last million years, caught in this cycle, which is the movement of thought. Within this area we have choice, we can go from one corner to the other and say, 'This is our choice, this is our movement of freedom', but it is always within this limited area of knowledge. So we are always functioning within the field of the known; and knowledge is always accompanied by ignorance because there is no complete knowledge about anything. So we are always in this contradictory state: knowledge and ignorance. Thought is incomplete, broken up, because knowledge can never be complete, so thought is limited, conditioned. And thought has created a thousand problems for us.

❖

KNOWLEDGE IS NECESSARY in a certain direction, and knowledge is the most dangerous thing that we have inwardly. You understand this? We are now accumulating a great deal of knowledge—about the universe, about the nature of everything, scientifically, archaeologically, and so on, we are collecting infinite knowledge. And that knowledge may be preventing us from acting as a total, complete human being. So that is one of our problems. That is, the computer can outstrip man in thinking, it can outlearn man, it can correct itself, it can learn to play chess masters and beat them after the fourth or fifth game. And they are now working on the ultimate intelligent machine.

❖

THE COMPUTER CAN have far greater knowledge than anybody. The size of a fingernail can contain the whole of the *Encyclopedia Britannica*, the whole of it. You understand? So what is man? Man has lived so far by the activity of his brain, keeping it active because he has struggled to survive, to accumulate knowledge skilfully to be secure, to have safety. Now the machine is taking all that over and what are you? The machine, the computer, with the robot, is building cars. The computer tells the robot what to do; and if the robot makes a mistake, the computer corrects it and the robot goes on. So what has become of man? What is the future of man if the machine can take over all the operations that thought does now, and do them far swifter, learn much more quickly, compete—do everything that man can do? Of course, it cannot look at the evening star and see the beauty of it, the extraordinary quietness, the steadiness, the immensity of that. The computer can't feel all that, but it may; they are working at it furiously.

So what is going to happen to our mind, to our brain? Our brains have lived so far by struggling to survive through knowledge. And when the machine takes all that over, what is going to happen to it? There are only two possibilities: Either man commits himself totally to outward entertainment, football, sports, or religious entertainment, going to the temple, you know, playing with all that stuff; or he turns inwardly, because the brain has infinite capacity, it is really infinite. That capacity is now used technologically, which the machine is going to take over. That capacity has been used to gather information, knowledge, whether scientific, political, social, or religious, and suddenly that brain's capacity is being taken over by the machine, and that is going to wither the brain. If I don't use my brain all the time, it will wither. So if the brain is not active, working, thinking—which the machine can do far better than the brain—then what is going to happen to the human brain? Either entertainment, or inquiry into oneself, which is infinite.

We have said that thought is the expression or the reaction of memory, and memory is the result of knowledge, which is experience. In this cycle man has been caught. In this area thought can invent gods, it can invent anything. And the machine has taken that over. So either I inquire into myself, which is infinite movement, or I plunge into entertainment. And most religions are entertainment, all the rituals, the pujas, are just a form of entertainment. So we have to inquire: What is religion? That is, we have to ask whether we can put our house in order—our house, the house inside us, the structure, the struggles, the pain, the anxiety, the loneliness, the aggression, the suffering, the pain, all that is such tremendous disorder in us. From that confusion, disorder, we try to bring about order out there, politically, economically, socially, all that, without having order inside. So to expect order out there without order here is impossible. Please see the logic of it. In this country, which is degenerating so fast—anarchy, total disorder, corruption, bribery, every form of dirty tricks that one can play from top to bottom, our house which we have created is in total disorder—and we are always asking for order out there; we say to the politicians, 'Please create order'. We never say the order must come first *here, in our house.* And only then will you have order out there.

20 June 1983:
From The Future of Humanity

Krishnamurti: Shouldn't we first distinguish between the brain and the mind?

David Bohm: Well, that distinction has been made, and it is not clear. Of course, there are several views. One is that the mind is just a function of the brain—that is the materialist view. There is another view which says mind and brain are two different things.

K: Yes, I think they are two different things.

DB: But there must be . . .

K: . . . a contact between the two, a relationship between the two.

DB: Yes, we don't necessarily imply any separation of the two.

K: No. First let's see the brain. I am really not an expert on the structure of the brain and all that kind of thing, but one can see within one, one can observe from one's own activity of the brain, that it is really like a computer which has been programmed and remembers.

DB: Certainly, a large part of the activity is that way, but one is not certain that all of it is that way.

K: No, and it is conditioned—by past generations, by society, by the newspapers, by the magazines, by all the activities and pressures from the outside. It is conditioned.

DB: Now, what do you mean by this conditioning?

K: The brain is programmed, it is made to conform to a certain pattern, it lives entirely on the past, modifying itself with the present, and going on.

DB: We have agreed that some of this conditioning is useful and necessary.

K: Of course.

DB: But the conditioning which determines the self, which determines the . . .

K: . . . the psyche. Let's call it for the moment the psyche, the self.

DB: The self, the psyche, that conditioning is what you are talking about. That may not only be unnecessary, but harmful.

K: Yes. The emphasis on the psyche, on giving importance to the self, is creating great damage in the world, because it is separative and therefore it is constantly in conflict, not only within itself, but with society, with the family, and so on.

DB: And it is also in conflict with nature.

K: With nature, with the whole universe.

DB: We have said that the conflict arose because . . .

K: . . . of division. . . .

DB: The division arising because thought is limited. Being based on this conditioning, on knowledge and memory, it is limited.

K: Yes, and experience is limited, therefore knowledge is limited; hence memory and thought. And the very structure and nature of the psyche is the movement of thought, the movement of thought in time.

DB: Yes, now I would like to ask a question. You have discussed the movement of thought, but it doesn't seem clear to me what is moving. You see, if I discuss the movement of my hand, that is a real movement. It is clear what is meant. But when we discuss the movement of thought, it seems to me we are discussing something which is a kind of illusion, because you have said that becoming is the movement of thought.

K: That is what I mean, the movement is becoming.

DB: But you are saying that movement is in some way illusory, aren't you?

K: Yes, of course.

DB: It is rather like the movement projected on the screen. We say that there are no objects moving across the screen, but the only real movement is the turning of the projector. Now, can we say that there is a real movement in the brain which is projecting all this, which is the conditioning?

K: That is what we want to find out. Let's discuss that a bit. We both agree, or see, that the brain is conditioned.

DB: We mean that really it has been impressed physically and chemically. . . .

K: And genetically, as well as psychologically.

DB: What is the difference between physically and psychologically?

K: Psychologically, the brain is centred in the self—right?—and the constant assertion of the self is the movement, the conditioning, an illusion.

DB: But there is some real movement happening inside. The brain, for example, is doing something. It has been conditioned physically and chemically, and something is happening physically and chemically when we are thinking of the self.

K: Are you asking whether the brain and the self are two different things?

DB: No, I am saying that the self is the result of conditioning the brain.

K: Yes, the self is conditioning the brain.

DB: But does the self exist?

K: No.

DB: But the conditioning of the brain, as I see it, is the involvement with an illusion which we call the self.

K: That's right. Can that conditioning be dissipated? That's the whole question.

DB: It really has to be dissipated in some physical, chemical, and neurophysiological sense.

K: Yes.

DB: Now, the first reaction of any scientific person would be that it looks unlikely that we could dissipate it by the sort of thing we are doing. You see, some scientists might feel that maybe we will discover drugs or new genetic changes or deep knowledge of the structure of the brain. In that way we could perhaps help to do something. I think that idea might be current among some people.

K: Will that change human behaviour?

DB: Why not? I think some people believe it might.

K: Wait a minute. That is the whole point. It might, which means in the future.

DB: Yes, it would take time to discover all this.

K: In the meantime, man is going to destroy himself

DB: They might hope that he will manage to discover it in time. They could also criticize what we are doing, saying what good can it do? You see, it doesn't seem to affect anybody, and certainly not in time to make a big difference.

K: We two are very clear about it. In what way does it affect humanity?

DB: Will it really affect mankind in time to save . . .

K: Obviously not.

DB: Then why should we be doing it?

K: Because this is the right thing to do. Independently. It has nothing to do with reward and punishment.

DB: Nor with goals. We do the right thing even though we don't know what the outcome will be?

K: That's right.

DB: Are you saying there is no other way?

K: We are saying there is no other way, that's right.

DB: Well, we should make that clear. For example, some psychologists would feel that by inquiring into this sort of thing, we could bring about an evolutionary transformation of consciousness.

K: We come back to the point that through time we hope to change consciousness. We question that.

DB: We have questioned that, and are saying that through time, inevitably we are all caught in becoming and illusion, and we will not know what we are doing.

K: That's right.

DB: Now, could we say that the same thing would hold even for those scientists who are trying to do it physically and chemically or structurally, that they themselves are still caught in this, and through time they are caught in trying to become better?

K: Yes, the experimenters and the psychologists and ourselves are all trying to become something.

DB: Yes, though it may not seem obvious at first. It may seem that the scientists are really just disinterested, unbiased observers, working on the problem. But underneath one feels there is the desire to become better on the part of the person who is inquiring in that way.

K: To become. Of course.

DB: He is not free of that.

K: That is just it.

DB: And that desire will give rise to self-deception and illusion, and so on.

K: So where are we now? Any form of becoming is an illusion, and becoming implies time, time for the psyche to change. But we are saying that time is not necessary.

DB: Now, that ties up with the other question of the mind and the brain. The brain is an activity in time, as a physical, chemical, complex process.

K: I think the mind is separate from the brain.

DB: What does *separate* mean? Are they in contact?

K: Separate in the sense that the brain is conditioned and the mind is not.

DB: Let's say the mind has a certain independence of the brain. Even if the brain is conditioned . . .

K: . . . the other is not.

DB: It need not be . . .

K: . . . conditioned.

DB: On what basis do you say that?

K: Let's not begin on what basis I say that.

DB: Well, what makes you say it?

K: As long as the brain is conditioned, it is not free, and the mind is free.

DB: Yes, that is what you are saying. But you see, the brain not being free means that it is not free to inquire in an unbiased way.

K: I will go into it. Let's inquire, What is freedom? Freedom to inquire, freedom to investigate. It is only in freedom that there is deep insight.

DB: Yes, that's clear, because if you are not free to inquire, or if you are biased, then you are limited, in an arbitrary way.

K: So as long as the brain is conditioned, its relationship to the mind is limited.

DB: We have the relationship of the brain to the mind, and also the other way round.

K: Yes, but the mind being free has a relationship to the brain.

DB: Yes, now we say the mind is free, in some sense, not subject to the conditioning of the brain.

K: Yes.

DB: What is the nature of the mind? Is the mind located inside the body, or is it in the brain?

K: No, it is nothing to do with the body or the brain.

DB: Has it to do with space or time?

K: Space—now wait a minute! It has to do with space and silence. These are the two factors of the . . .

DB: But not time?

K: Not time. Time belongs to the brain.

DB: You say space and silence; now, what kind of space? It is not the space in which we see life moving.

K: Space. Let's look at it the other way. Thought can invent space.

DB: In addition, we have the space that we see. But thought can invent all kinds of space.

K: And space from here to there.

DB: Yes, the space through which we move is that way.

K: Space also between two noises, two sounds.

DB: The interval between two sounds.

K: Yes, the interval between two noises, two thoughts, two notes, space between two people.

DB: Yes, space between the walls.

K: And so on. But that kind of space is not the space of the mind.

DB: You say it is not limited?

K: That's right, but I didn't want to use the word limited.

DB: But it is implied. That kind of space is not in the nature of being bounded by something.

K: No, it is not bounded by the psyche.

DB: But is it bounded by anything?

K: No. So can the brain, with all its cells conditioned, can those cells radically change?

DB: We have often discussed this. It is not certain that all the cells are conditioned. For example, some people think that only some or a small part of the cells are being used, and that the others are just inactive, dormant.

K: Hardly used at all, or just touched occasionally.

DB: Just touched occasionally. But those cells that are conditioned, whatever they may be, evidently dominate consciousness now.

K: Yes, can those cells be changed? We are saying that they can, through insight; insight being out of time, not the result of remembrance, an intuition, or desire, or hope. It is nothing to do with any time and thought.

DB: Yes, now is insight of the mind, is it of the nature of mind, an activity of mind?

K: Yes.

DB: Therefore you are saying that mind can act in the matter of the brain.

K: Yes, we said that earlier.

DB: But, you see, this point, how mind is able to act in matter, is difficult.

K: It is able to act on the brain. For instance, take any crisis or problem. The root meaning of problem is, as you know, 'something thrown at you'. And we meet it with all the remembrance of the past, with a bias, and so on. And therefore the problem multiplies itself. You may solve one problem, but in the very solution of one particular problem, other problems arise, as happens in politics, and so on. Now, to approach the problem, or to have perception of it without any past memories and thoughts interfering or projecting . . .

DB: That implies that perception also is of the mind. . . .

K: Yes, that's right.

DB: Are you saying that the brain is a kind of instrument of the mind?

K: An instrument of the mind when the brain is not self-centred.

DB: All the conditioning may be thought of as the brain exciting itself, and keeping itself going just from the programme, this occupies all of its capacities.

K: All our days, yes.

DB: The brain is rather like a radio receiver which can generate its own noise, but would not pick up a signal.

K: Not quite, let's go into this a little. Experience is always limited. I may blow up that experience into something fantastic, and then set up a shop to sell my experience, but that experience is limited. And so knowledge is always limited, and this knowledge is operating in the brain, this knowledge is the brain. And thought is also part of the brain, and thought is limited. So the brain is operating in a very, very small area.

DB: Yes, what prevents it from operating in a broader area, in an unlimited area?

K: Thought.

DB: But it seems to me the brain is running on its own, from its own programme.

K: Yes, like a computer.

DB: Essentially, what you are asking is that the brain should really be responding to the mind.

K: It can only respond if it is free from the limited, from thought, which is limited.

DB: So the programme does not then dominate it. You see, we are still going to need that programme.

K: Of course. We need it for . . .

DB: . . . for many things. But is intelligence from the mind?

K: Yes, intelligence is the mind.

DB: Is the mind.

K: We must go into something else. Because compassion is related to intelligence, there is no intelligence without compassion. And compassion can only be when there is love which is completely free from all remembrances, personal jealousies, and so on.

DB: Is all that compassion, love, also of the mind?

K: Of the mind. You cannot be compassionate if you are attached to any particular experience or any particular ideal.

DB: Yes, that is again the programme.

K: Yes, for instance, there are those people who go out to various poverty-ridden countries and work, work, work, and they call that compassion. But they are attached or tied to a particular form of religious belief, and therefore their action is merely pity or sympathy, it is not compassion.

DB: Yes, I understand that we have here two things which can be somewhat independent. There is the brain and the mind, though they make contact. Then we say that intelligence and compassion come from beyond the brain. Now I would like to go into the question of how they are making contact.

K: Ah! Contact can only exist between the mind and the brain when the brain is quiet.

DB: Yes, that is the requirement for making it, the brain has to be quiet.

K: Quiet is not a trained quietness, not a self-conscious, meditative, desire for silence. It is a natural outcome of understanding one's own conditioning.

DB: And one can see that if the brain is quiet, it could listen to something deeper?

K: That's right. Then if it is quiet, it is related to the mind. Then the mind can function through the brain. . . .

K: So can we remain with 'what is', not with 'what should be', 'what must be', not invent ideals, and so on?

DB: Yes, but could we return to the question of the mind and the brain? Now we are saying that is not a division.

K: Oh no, that is not a division.

DB: They are in contact, is that right?

K: We said, there is contact between the mind and the brain when the brain is silent and has space.

DB: So we are saying that although they are in contact and not divided at all, the mind can still have a certain independence of the conditioning of the brain.

K: Now, let's be careful! Suppose my brain is conditioned, for example, programmed as a Hindu, and my whole life and action are conditioned by the idea that I am a Hindu. Mind obviously has no relationship with that conditioning.

DB: You are using the word *mind*, not 'my' mind.

K: Mind, it is not 'mine'.

DB: It is universal or general.

K: Yes, and it is not 'my' brain either.

DB: No, but there is a particular brain, this brain or that brain. Would you say that there is a particular mind?

K: No.

DB: That is an important difference. You are saying mind is really universal.

K: Mind is universal—if we can use that ugly word.

DB: Unlimited and undivided.

K: It is unpolluted, not polluted by thought.

DB: But I think for most people there will be difficulty in saying how we know anything about this mind. We only know that 'my' mind is the first feeling—right?

K: You cannot call it your mind, you only have your brain, which is conditioned. You can't say, 'It is my mind'.

DB: But whatever is going on inside I feel is mine, and it is very different from what is going on inside somebody else.

K: No, I question whether it is different.

DB: At least it seems different.

K: Yes, I question whether it is different, what is going on inside me as a human being, and you as another human being. We both go through all kinds of problems, suffering, fear, anxiety, loneliness, and so on. We have our dogmas, beliefs, superstitions. And everybody has these.

DB: We can say it is all very similar, but it seems as if each one of us is isolated from the other.

K: By thought. My thought has created the belief that I am different from you, because my body is different from yours, my face is different from yours. We extend that same thing into the psychological area.

DB: But now if we said that division is an illusion, perhaps?

K: No, not perhaps! It is.

DB: It is an illusion. All right, although it is not obvious when a person first looks at it.

K: Of course.

DB: In reality even brain is not divided, because we are saying that we are all not only basically similar but really connected. And then we say beyond all that is mind, which has no division at all.

K: It is unconditioned.

DB: Yes, it would almost seem to imply, then, that in so far as a person feels he is a separate being, he has very little contact with mind.

K: Quite right, that is what we said.

DB: No mind.

K: That is why it is very important to understand not the mind, but our conditioning. And whether our conditioning, human conditioning, can ever be dissolved. That is the real issue.

❖

K: Let's take a problem, then it is easier to understand. Take the problem of suffering. Human beings have suffered endlessly, through wars, through physical disease, and through wrong relationship with each other. Now, can that end?

DB: I would say the difficulty of ending that is that it is on the programme, we are conditioned to this whole thing.

K: Yes, now that has been going on for centuries.

DB: So it is very deep.

K: Very, very deep. Now, can that suffering end?

DB: It cannot end by an action of the brain.

K: By thought.

DB: Because the brain is caught in suffering, and it cannot take an action to end its own suffering.

K: Of course it cannot. That is why thought cannot end it. Thought has created it.

DB: Yes, thought has created it, and anyway it is unable to get hold of it.

K: Thought has created the wars, the misery, the confusion. And thought has become prominent in human relationship.

DB: Yes, but I think people might agree with that and still think that just as thought can do bad things, it can do good things.

K: No, thought cannot do good or bad, it is thought, limited.

DB: Thought cannot get hold of this suffering. That is, this suffering being in the physical and chemical conditioning of the brain, thought has no way of even knowing what it is.

K: I mean, I lose my son and I am . . .

DB: Yes, but by thinking, I don't know what is going on inside me. I can't change the suffering inside because thinking will not show me what it is. Now you are saying intelligence is perception.

K: But we are asking, can suffering end? That is the problem.

DB: Yes, and it is clear that thinking cannot end it.

K: Thought cannot do it. That is the point. If I have an insight into it . . .

DB: Now, this insight will be through the action of the mind, through intelligence and attention.

K: When there is that insight, intelligence wipes away suffering.

DB: You are saying, therefore, that there is a contact from mind to matter which removes the whole physical, chemical structure that keeps us going on with suffering.

K: That's right, in that ending there is a mutation in the brain cells.

DB: Yes, and that mutation just wipes out the whole structure that makes you suffer.

K: That's right. Therefore it is as if I have been going along with a certain tradition, I suddenly change that tradition, and there is a change in the whole brain; it has been going north, now it goes east.

DB: Of course, this is a radical notion from the point of view of traditional ideas in science because, if we accept that mind is different from matter, then people would find it hard to say that mind would actually ...

K: Would you put it that mind is pure energy?

DB: Well, we could put it that way, but matter is energy too.

K: But matter is limited, thought is limited.

DB: But we are saying that the pure energy of mind is able to reach into the limited energy of matter?

K: Yes, that's right, and change the limitation.

DB: Remove some of the limitation.

K: When there is a deep issue, problem, or challenge which you are facing.

DB: We could also add that all the traditional ways of trying to do this cannot work. . . .

K: They haven't worked.

DB: Well, that is not enough. We have to say, because people still might hope they could, that they actually cannot.

K: They cannot.

DB: Because thought cannot get at its own physical, chemical basis in the cells, and do anything about those cells.

K: Yes, thought cannot bring about a change in itself.

DB: And yet practically everything that mankind has been trying to do is based on thought. There is a limited area, of course, where that is all right, but we cannot do anything about the future of humanity from that usual approach.

K: When one listens to the politicians, who are so very active in the world, they are creating problem after problem, and to them thought, ideals are the most important things.

DB: Generally speaking, nobody knows of anything else.

K: Exactly. We are saying that the old instrument which is thought is worn out, except in certain areas.

DB: It never was adequate, except in those areas.

K: Of course.

DB: And, as far as history goes, man has always been in trouble.

K: Man has always been in trouble, in turmoil, in fear. And facing all the confusion of the world, can there be a solution to all this?

DB: That comes back to the question I would like to repeat. It seems there are a few people who are talking about it, and think perhaps they know, or perhaps they meditate, and so on. But how is that going to affect this vast current of mankind?

K: Probably very little. But why will it affect this? It might, or it might not. But then one puts that question: What is the use of it?

DB: Yes, that's the point. I think there is an instinctive feeling that makes one put the question.

K: But I think that is the wrong question.

DB: You see, the first instinct is to say, 'What can we do to stop this tremendous catastrophe?'

K: Yes. But if each one of us, whoever listens, sees the truth that thought, in its activity both externally and inwardly, has created a terrible mess, great suffering, then one must inevitably ask is there an ending to all this? If thought cannot end it, what will? What is the new instrument that will put an end to all this misery? You see, there is a new instrument which is the mind, which is intelligence. But the difficulty is also that people won't listen to all this. Both the scientists and the ordinary laymen like us have come to definite conclusions, and they won't listen.

DB: Yes, well, that is what I had in mind when I said that a few people don't seem to have much effect.

K: Of course. I think, after all, a few people *have* changed the world—whether good or bad is not the point. Hitler and also the Communists have changed it, but they have gone to the same pattern again. Physical revolution has never psychologically changed the human state.

DB: Do you think it is possible that a certain number of brains coming in contact with mind in this way will be able to have an effect on mankind, which is beyond just the immediate, obvious effect of their communication? I mean, obviously, whoever does this may communicate in the ordinary way and it will have a small effect, but now this is a possibility of something entirely different.

K: Yes, that's right. But how do you convey—I have often thought about this—this subtle and very complex issue to a person who is steeped in tradition, who is conditioned, and won't even take time to listen, to consider?

DB: Well, that is the question. You see, you could say that this conditioning cannot be absolute, cannot be an absolute block, or else there would be no way out at all. But the conditioning may be thought to have some sort of permeability.

K: I mean, after, all, the pope won't listen to us, but the pope has tremendous influence.

DB: Is it possible that every person has something he can listen to, if it could be found?

K: If he has a little patience. Who will listen? The politicians won't listen, the idealists won't listen, the totalitarians won't listen, the deeply steeped religious people won't listen. So perhaps a so-called ignorant person, not highly educated or conditioned in his professional career, or by money, the poor man who says, 'I am suffering, please let's end that' . . .

DB: But he doesn't listen either, you see. He wants to get a job.

K: Of course. He says, 'Feed me first'. We have been through all this for the last sixty years. The poor man won't listen, the rich man won't listen, the learned won't listen, and the deeply dogmatic religious believers won't listen. So perhaps it is like a wave in the world; it might catch somebody. I think it is a wrong question to say, 'Does it affect?'

DB: Yes, all right. We will say that that brings in time, and that is becoming. It brings in the psyche in the process of becoming again.

K: Yes. But if you say . . . it must affect mankind . . .

DB: Are you proposing that it affects mankind through the mind directly, rather than through . . .

K: Yes, it may not show immediately in action.

DB: You are taking very seriously what you said about the mind being universal, not located in our ordinary space, not being separate . . .

K: Yes, but there is a danger in saying this, that the mind is universal. That is what some people say of the mind, and it has become a tradition.

DB: One can turn it into an idea, of course.

K: That is just the danger of it, that is what I am saying.

DB: Yes, but really the question is, we have to come directly in contact with this to make it real. Right?

K: That's it. We can only come into contact with it when the self is not. To put it very simply, when the self is not, there is beauty, silence, space; then that intelligence, which is born of compassion, operates through the brain. It is very simple.

Saanen, 25 July 1983

Questioner: Could we speak about the brain and the mind? Thinking takes place materially in the brain cells. That is, thinking is a material process. If thinking stops and there is perception without thought, what happens to the material brain? You seem to say that mind has its place outside the brain, but where does the movement of pure perception take place if not somewhere in the brain? And how is it possible for mutation to take place in the brain cells if pure perception has no connection in the brain?

Krishnamurti: Have you got the question? First, the questioner says to differentiate between the mind and the brain. Then he asks if perception is purely outside the brain, which means thought is not the movement of perception. And he asks, if perception takes place outside the brain, which is the thinking process, remembering process, then what happens to the brain cells themselves, which are conditioned by the past? And will there be a mutation in the brain cells if perception is outside? Is this clear?

So let's begin with the brain and the mind. The brain is a material function, it is a muscle—right?—like the heart, and the brain cells contain all the memories. Please, I am not a brain specialist, nor have I studied the experts, but I have lived a long time now and I have watched a great deal, not only the reaction of others—what they say, what they think, what they want to tell me—

but also I have watched how the brain reacts. So the brain has evolved through time from the single cell, taking millions of years, until it reached the ape and went on another million years until man could stand and so ultimately the human brain. The human brain is contained within the skull but it can go beyond itself. You can sit here and think of your country, or your home, you are instantly there—in thought, not physically. The brain has extraordinary capacity, technologically, it has done the most extraordinary things.

So the brain has extraordinary capacity. That brain has been conditioned by the limitation of language, not language itself, but the limitation of language; it has been conditioned by the climate it lives in, by the food eaten, by the society in which it lives—and that society has been created by the brain. That society is not different from the activities of the brain. It has been conditioned by millions of years of experience, of accumulated knowledge based on that experience, which is tradition. I am British, you are German, he is a Hindu, he is a black man, he is this, he is that—all the nationalistic division, which is tribal division—and the religious conditioning. So the brain is conditioned. The brain has extraordinary capacity, but it has been conditioned and therefore it is limited. It is not limited in the technological world, computers and so on, but it is very, very limited with regard to the psyche. People have said, 'Know yourself'—from the Greeks, from the ancient Hindus, and so on. They study the psyche in another but they never study their own psyche. The psychologists, the philosophers, the experts, never study themselves. They study rats, rabbits, pigeons, monkeys, and so on, but they never say, 'I am going to look at myself. I am ambitious, greedy, envious, I compete with my neighbour, with my fellow scientists. It is the same psyche that has existed for thousands of years, though technologically we are marvellous outwardly. But inwardly we are very primitive—right?

So the brain is limited, primitive, in the world of the psyche. Now, can that limitation be broken down? Can that limitation, which is the self, the ego, the me, self-centred concern, can all that be wiped away? Which means the brain is then unconditioned—

you understand what I am saying? Then it has no fear. Now, most of us live in fear, are anxious, frightened of what is going to happen, frightened of death, of a dozen things. Can all that be completely wiped away and be fresh? So that the brain is free and its relationship to the mind is then entirely different. That means to see that one has no shadow of the self. And that is extraordinarily arduous, to see the 'me' doesn't enter into any field. The self hides in many ways, under every stone, the self can hide in compassion, going to India and looking after poor people, because the self is attached to some idea, faith, conclusion, belief, which makes me compassionate because I love Jesus or Krishna, and I go up to heaven. The self has many masks, the mask of meditation, the mask of achieving the highest, the mask that I am enlightened, that 'I know of what I speak'. All this concern about humanity is another mask. So one has to have an extraordinary, subtle, quick brain to see where it is hiding. It requires great attention, watching, watching, watching. You won't do all this. Probably you are all too lazy or too old and say, 'For God's sake, all this isn't worth it, let me alone'. But if one really wants to go into this very deeply, one has to watch like a hawk every movement of thought, every movement of reaction, so the brain can be free from its conditioning. The speaker is speaking for himself, not for anybody else. He may be deceiving himself, he may be trying to pretend to be something or other—you understand? He may be, you don't know. So have a great deal of scepticism, doubt, question, not accepting what others say.

So when there is no conditioning of the brain, it no longer degenerates. As you get older and older—perhaps not you—but as people generally get older and older, their brain begins to wear out, they lose their memories, they behave in a peculiar way, you know all that. Degeneration is not merely in America, degeneration takes place in the brain first. And when the brain is completely free of the self and therefore no longer conditioned, then we can ask: What is the mind?

The ancient Hindus inquired into the mind, and they have posited various statements. But wiping all that out, not depending on anyone however ancient, however traditional, what is the mind?

❖

OUR BRAIN IS constantly in conflict, and therefore it is disorder. Such a brain cannot understand what the mind is. The mind—not my mind, *the* mind, the mind that has created the universe, the mind that has created the cell, that mind which is pure energy and intelligence—can have a relationship to the brain only when the brain is free; but if the brain is conditioned, there is no relationship. You don't have to believe all this. So intelligence is the essence of that mind, not the intelligence of thought, not the intelligence of disorder. But it is pure order, pure intelligence, and therefore it is pure compassion. And that mind has a relationship with the brain when the brain is free.

Are you listening to yourself, or are you just listening to me? Are you doing both? Are you watching your own reactions, how your brain works? That is, action, reaction, back and forth, back and forth, which means you are not listening. You are only listening when this action, reaction, stops; just pure listening. Look, the sea is in constant movement. The tide is coming in, the tide is going out. This is its action. And human beings are also in this action, re- action. Reaction in me produces another reaction, and so back and forth. Therefore, when there is that movement back and forth, there is naturally no quietness. In quietness you can hear the truth or the falseness, not when you are back and forth, back and forth. At least see intellectually, logically, that if there is constant move- ment, you are not listening. How can you listen! Only when there is absolute silence can you listen. Right? See the logic of it. And is it possible to stop this movement back and forth? The speaker says it is possible when you have studied yourself, when you have gone into yourself very, very deeply. Understand yourself—then you can say the movement has really stopped.

And the questioner asks: As the mind is outside, not con- tained in the brain, how can perception, which takes place only when there is no activity of thought, bring about a mutation in the brain cells, which are a material process?

Look, keep it very simple. This is one of our difficulties: we never look at a complex thing very simply. This is a very, very complex question, but we must begin very simply to understand something very vast. So let's begin simply. Traditionally, you have pursued a certain path, religiously, economically, socially, morally, and so on, in a certain direction all your life. Suppose I have done this. You come along and say, 'Look, the way you are going leads nowhere, it will bring you much more trouble, you will keep everlastingly killing each other, you will have tremendous economic difficulty', and he gives me logical reasons, examples, and so on. But I say, 'No, sorry, this is my way of doing things'. And I keep going that way. Most people do, ninety-nine per cent of people keep going that way, including the gurus, including the philosophers, including the newly achieved, enlightened people. And you come along and say, 'Look, that is a dangerous path, don't go there. Turn and go in another direction entirely'. And you convince me, you show me the logic, the reason, the sanity of it, and I turn and go in a totally different direction. What has taken place? I have been going in one direction all my life, you come along and say, 'Don't go there, it is dangerous, it leads nowhere. You will have more trouble, more aches, more problems. Go in another direction, things will be entirely different'. And I accept your logic, your statements sanely, and I move in another direction. What has happened to the brain? Keep it simple. Going in that direction, suddenly move in the other direction, the brain cells have themselves changed. You understand? I have broken the tradition. It is as simple as that. But the tradition is so strong, it has all its roots in my present existence and you are asking me to do something which I rebel against, therefore I do not listen. Or, instead, I listen to find out if what you are saying is true or false. I want to know the truth of the matter, not my wishes, my pleasures, I want to know the truth of it, therefore being serious I listen with all my being and I see you are quite right. I have moved—right? In that movement there is a change in the brain cells. It is as simple as that.

Look, suppose I am a practising Catholic or Hindu and you come and tell me, 'Look, don't be silly, all that is nonsense. They are just traditions, words without much meaning, though the words have accumulated meaning'. You understand? So you point this out and I see what you say is the truth, I move, I am free from that conditioning, therefore there is a change, a mutation in the brain. Or I have been brought up, we have all been brought up, to live with fear. We are all brought up, not only fear of something, but fear. And you tell me it can end and instinctively I say, 'Show it, let's go together, find out'. I want to find out if what you are saying is true or false, whether fear can really end. So I spend time, I discuss with you, I want to find out, learn, so my brain is active to find out, not to be told what to do. So the moment I begin to inquire, work, look, watch the whole movement of fear, then I accept it and say, 'Well, I like to live in fear', or I move away from it. When you see that, there is a change in the brain cells.

It is so simple if you could only look at this thing very simply. There is a mutation—to make it a little more complex—in the very brain cells, not through any effort, not through will or through any motive, when there is perception. Perception is when there is observation without a movement of thought, when there is absolute silence of memory, which is time, which is thought. To look at something without the past. Do it. Look at the speaker without all the remembrance that you have accumulated about him. Watch him, or watch your father, your mother, your husband, wife, girl, and so on—it doesn't matter what—watch without any past remembrance and hurt and guilt coming into being. Just watch. When you so watch without any prejudice, then there is freedom from that which has been.

Brockwood Park, 30 August 1983: From The World of Peace

ALL THAT WE are saying is: Thought is necessary in certain areas, it is not necessary in others. That requires a great deal of observation, attention, care, to find out where thought is not necessary. Right? But we are so impatient, we want to get at it quickly, like taking a pill for a headache. But we never find out what is the cause of the headache.

Brockwood Park, 25 August 1984

IS THE SPEAKER telling a fairy story? Or is he describing or stating facts? And those facts are: There is no love. One may talk about love, 'Oh I love her so much'—you know all that business very well. And in that there is dependence, attachment, fear, antagonism, gradually jealousy, the whole machinery of human relationship with all its agony, fear, loss, gain, despair, depression. How can all this end so that we have real relationship with each other, between man and woman? Is it knowledge of each other? Do look at it, please consider it. I know my wife—which means what? When you say, 'I know her, she is my wife', what does that mean? Or my girlfriend, or whoever it is. Is it all the pleasure, the pain, the anxiety, the jealousy, the struggle with occasional flashes of tenderness? Is all that part of love? Is attachment love? I am asking these questions, go into it, find out. One is attached to one's wife, tremendous attachment. What is implied in that attachment? I cannot stand by myself, therefore I must depend on somebody, whether it is a wife or husband or some psychiatrist or guru, and all that tommyrot! Where there is attachment, there is fear of loss, a sense of deep possessiveness, and therefore it breeds fear. You know all this.

So can we look at the fact of our relationship and discover for ourselves the place of thought in relationship? As we said, thought is limited, which is a fact. If in our relationship thought is a prominent factor, then in that relationship that factor is limiting, so our relationship with each other is limited and therefore inevitably must breed conflict. There is the conflict between the Arab and the Israeli, because each is clinging to his own conditioning, which means being programmed; each human being is programmed like a computer. I know it sounds cruel but it is a fact. When you are told you are an Indian from childhood, belonging to a certain social or religious category, you are conditioned, and for the rest of your life you are Indian, or British, French, German, or Russian, or whatever it is. So there it is.

So our relationship, which should be the most extraordinary thing in life, is one of the causes of wastage of our life. We are wasting our life in our relationships. When you really see this is a fact, give your attention to it, that is, understand very deeply the nature of thought and time, which has nothing whatsoever to do with love. Thought and time is a movement in the brain. And love is outside the brain. Please go into this very carefully because what is inside the skull is very important, how it functions, what are its blockages, why it is limited, why there is this perpetual sense of chattering, thought after thought, a series of associations, reactions, responses, the whole storehouse of memory, and memory obviously is not love. Therefore love cannot be, is not, inside the brain, the skull. And when we merely live inside the skull all the time, all the days of our life, thinking, thinking, thinking, problem after problem, which is to live inside limitation, that must inevitably breed conflict and misery.

Madras, 2 January 1983:
From Mind Without Measure

WHAT IS COMPASSION?—not the definition that you can look up in a dictionary. What is the relationship between love and compassion, or are they the same movement? When we use the word 'relationship', it implies a duality, a separation, but we are asking what place love has in compassion, or is love the highest expression of compassion? How can you be compassionate if you belong to any religion, follow any guru, believe in something, believe in your scriptures, and so on, are attached to a conclusion? When you accept your guru, you have come to a conclusion; or when you strongly believe in God or a saviour, this or that, can there be compassion? You may do social work, help the poor out of pity, sympathy, charity, but is all that love and compassion? In understanding the nature of love, having that quality which is mind in the heart, that is intelligence. *Intelligence is the understanding or discovering of what love is. Intelligence has nothing whatsoever to do with thought, with cleverness, with knowledge.* You may be very clever in your studies, in your job, in being able to argue very cleverly, reasonably, but that is not intelligence. Intelligence goes with love and compassion, and you cannot come upon that intelligence as an individual. Compassion is not yours or mine, any more than thought is yours or mine.

When there is intelligence, there is no 'me' and 'you'. And intelligence does not abide in your heart or your mind. That intelligence which is supreme is everywhere. It is that intelligence that moves the earth and the heavens and the stars, because that is compassion.

Sources and Acknowledgments

From the report of the public talk in Seattle, 23 July 1950, in volume VI, *The Collected Works of J. Krishnamurti* copyright © 1991 The Krishnamurti Foundation of America.

From the report of the public talk in London, 7 April 1952, in volume VI, *The Collected Works of J. Krishnamurti* copyright © 1991 The Krishnamurti Foundation of America.

From the report of the public talk at Rajghat, 23 January 1955, in volume VIII, *The Collected Works of J. Krishnamurti* copyright © 1991 The Krishnamurti Foundation of America.

From the report of the public talk at Rajghat, 6 February 1955, in volume VIII, *The Colleted Works of J. Krishnamurti* copyright © 1991 The Krishnamurti Foundation of America.

From the report of the public talk at Ojai, 21 August 1955, in volume IX, *The Collected Works of J. Krishnamurti* copyright © 1991 The Krishnamurti Foundation of America.

From the report of the public talk at Rajghat, 25 December 1955, in volume IX, *The Collected Works of J. Krishnamurti* copyright © 1991 The Krishnamurti Foundation of America.

From the report of the public talk in Bombay, 28 February 1965, in volume XV, *The Collected Works of J. Krishnamurti* copyright © 1992 The Krishnamurti Foundation of America.

From *The Only Revolution* copyright © 1970 J. Krishnamurti.

From the recording of the public talk at Saanen, 23 July 1970, copyright © 1970/1993 Krishnamurti Foundation Trust, Ltd.